NOT the WALTONS

The Making of a Boomer

Glen P. Aylward

Springfield, IL
Gpapsych@aol.com
Gpapsych7@me.com

ISBN: 1490423605
ISBN 13: 9781490423609

Love and thanks to my family for their support and encouragement. At least they now understand, to some degree, why I act the way I do. Thanks also to my old friends and acquaintances for their participation in my life experiences. Your names have been altered to protect your anonymity (but you know who you are).

CONTENTS

NOT the WALTONS:
The Making of a Boomer

Foreword

Several factors influenced me to write this book, which some may consider an amalgam of Dave Barry meets 'A Christmas Story', sprinkled with a touch of the Thunderbolt Kid—the aggregate providing a rather unique perspective on life. First I'm 60+ years old, and at that age, people become retrospective—if they can remember enough to actually *be* retrospective. As such I'm a bona-fide, card-carrying boomer, one of the 76 million or so individuals born between 1946 and 1964 during an extended flurry of post-war revelry. Second, I'm a clinical psychologist, and as such I practice on the premise that early experiences tend to mold the adult personality— for better or worse. So, I'm a semi-old, bona-fide card-carrying AARP member (eligible for the highly sought after early bird senior meal specials), who is supposed to diagnose, give advice, and interpret what causes people to act the way they do. However, in my training I was taught to *always* make sure that any of my own issues or biases didn't affect how I dealt with patients. In order to do that, I had to take a long hard look at my own early experiences, more specifically, family, peer group and neighborhood interactions—the veritable building blocks of one's adult personality. Third, in retrospect, I had some rather unique, actual experiences, these providing a basis for the book.

Herein, I have included a variety of recollections that were rekindled by peculiar client encounters, not in any particular order, either time-wise or importance-wise. Maybe not wise in any way. Nonetheless, they did, undoubtedly, help define my adult psyche and also those of my collaborators.

What I found most amazing was how an interaction with a patient, whether it be an empathic interlude or a few rounds of verbal fisticuffs, conjured up some pretty vivid memories. Repressed? Maybe. Misfiled? Likely. Unusual? Positively. Re-discovering some of these memories was metaphorically like defragging a computer (something like rear-ranging the clutter on the office desk). One's mind is like a computer to some degree, you know—buzzing, clicking, conflicting, churning out error messages, flickering, and, most of the time, on screen saver mode. Of course, there also is the occasional crashing and mad scramble to re-boot.

Many of the vignettes herein are universal experiences. Every ethnic group has its own themes—as does each section of the coun-try- in my case, the East coast. New Jersey, to be exact. Each genera-tion also is unique and this book addresses growing up in the 50's and 60's. Everyone has a cousin Joey story—or an Aunt Nancy. Different ethnicities, different names, but similar stories, nonetheless. It's a sort of a collective unconscious (in Jungian terms), common to the brotherhood or sisterhood of man; in this case, the brother- or sister-hood of the Baby Boomer Nation. On second thought, it might be a collective, *neurotic* unconscious—but it could offer an explanation for *why-in-the-heck-am-I-remembering-this-again?*

In at least part of the book any resemblance to actual persons, living or deceased, is purely coincidental—unless it's caused by repression or lying.

CHAPTER 1

Session 1: Time with Ida

"Whaddya' mean I'm hostile?"

"Your veins are sticking out."

"Whaddaya' mean my veins are sticking out?"

"I mean you're hostile and your veins are sticking out of your neck and forehead."

"My veins always stick out!"

"Not like that Mrs. Plotsky they're *really big!*. Besides, you're sort of growling."

"Growling is it? Now you're calling me a dog. Up your ass doc!"

"See, you *are* hostile!"

"You're the asshole who's making me hostile! I'm plain, old-time, flat-out pissed off!"

"So you admit you're pissed off?"

"Damn straight I'm pissed off!"

"At whom?"

"At you, meathead! What?? Are you a moron or something?"

"Anyone else?"

"What do you mean anyone else? *You're* the one who's telling me I'm barking!"

"Growling."

"Whatever—you remind me so much of my older brother-Mr. Fancy pants, Joseph. He always pissed me off—still does!"

'Aha'—I subtly scribbled some notes-'making progress, a real break-through—some insight-transference-her brother used to make her angry. He left a nerve exposed. Explains her short fuse and anger toward males.' A mental note was to the effect of 'pity her poor husband.'

Dear Mrs. Ida Plotsky—50-ish, rather round, always in dark clothes, wearing a fur-trimmed coat and furry hat that looks like she accidentally grabbed the cat off the coat rack and put it on her head on the way out.

"Hmmm, next week we'll have to talk about Joseph."

"Why in the hell would I want to talk about that putz?"

"Because he makes you angry."

"YOU make me angry!!"

"Well we can't talk about me, besides, I'm just facilitating the release of some of the anger you're holding inside. I think you're really mad at Joseph!"

"You're nuts!! You're an idiot! Besides that you're a friggin' moron!"

"Idiot? Moron? Now, now, (keep smiling, be kind and neutral I told myself—nothing personal)… Our time's about up, shall we set up the usual appointment for one o'clock next Thursday?"

"Hey-you piss me off and then tell me to leave!?"

"No, Mrs. Plotsky, you know I'd like to talk with you longer, but we only have 45 minutes and it's time to stop."

"And you charge me an arm and a leg for this shit!"

"Now, now."

"And quit sayin' 'now, now'!"

Mrs. Plotsky gathered her coat, purse with a string of beads hanging out (I recognized them immediately to be—*Rosary Beads*!), twisted tissues, and her umbrella, and shuffled out, muttering something inaudible. At least her veins had subsided back to baseline. Her hat seemed to be on sideways—if it had a sideways. I jotted some notes to document the major issues of the day and to jog my memory next week regarding the focus of the session.

I wrote some additional notes: '1/8/12—Patient really "ticked off"— Sees therapist as brother figure. Transfers anger directed at brother to therapist. Plan is to see what brother did to make her angry. Explore how she deals with anger.'

I flipped backward a page and read a previous note—'12/31/11— patient still rather belligerent—seems like it's me she's angry at. Plan is to explore that further.'

And I flipped back yet another page—'12/24/11—Patient not in Christmas spirit—really volatile, definitely angry...no ho, ho, ho'

I was musing about Mrs. Plotsky's consistency in terms of affect when there was a knock on the office door. Connie, the receptionist, came in, apologizing for the intrusion. Connie was a 60-ish woman, whose overall physical composition resembled a square. Her piercing blue eyes were accented by her tightly pulled-back, gray hair that culminated in a bun. She always wore a sweater, even in the summer. The tightness of the hair weave always seemed to give her a built-in face lift and I secretly bet that she used some type of tourniquet to achieve the desired effect.

"Dr. Wayward, do you know that Mrs. Plotsky showed her teeth and seemed to *growl* at me? Does the poor woman have Tourette's? And her *veins*!!!!"

"Connie, you know I can't discuss patients...."

I now had a mental image of Mrs. Plotsky leaning over the desk and growling,—perhaps she's a ventriloquist, speaking through that critter she wore on her head— Connie glaring back so hard (with eye widening aided by the hair tourniquet) it would seem like lasers were going in Mrs. P's eyeballs and turning her brain to jello. Connie was by far the best attack receptionist around, taking nothing from anyone—growlers included! I had a vision of two pit bulls sniffing, circling, and waiting for the other to make some type of fatal mistake.

"She said you were a pain in the butt, but that you probably knew what you were doing."

"Thanks, Connie."

That was as close as you got to receiving a compliment from Mrs. P, I guess. As I waited to see the next client I caught myself daydreaming. Come to think of it, my older brother, Philip, still tends to tick me off. I don't growl though—I guess I keep it in—suppressed, repressed or whatever. Maybe that's why I always forget to send him a birthday card- or consistently buy him Christmas presents that are the wrong size, just so he'd have to take them back. His wife, the Matrimony Nazi, sure as hell wouldn't! Philip's compulsiveness would cause him to return the gift the day after Christmas, and leave him vulnerable to hand-to-hand mortal combat with the merchandise-return guerrillas. Not to mention the never ending return lines from hell. This is especially sweet because he loathes shopping in general. Could that also be why I 'occasionally' used to take a homework paper or two out of his backpack? How delightful it was to hear my parents scream at him something about the fact that if he indeed DID his homework why in the hell didn't he turn it in? How stupid is that? This was usually followed by a consequence (namely, grounding or loss of television). That typically was an opportune time for me to show my parents an 'A' paper in something or other that I had been saving for such an occasion (an "I love you mom and dad" home-made card really rounded out the bill—a proverbial dagger to Philip's heart). A mass produced stash of these cards was cleverly concealed under my bed, ready to be activated at a moment's notice. I wondered if Ida Plotsky did the same type of stuff in her childhood. I'd bet she was more aggressive than passive—probably used a bat, although I'm sure her right hook was formidable. Maybe even a left-right combination. Then again, maybe her brother took her homework out of *her* backpack. Or schoolbag—I can visualize her with this huge, black schoolbag (with fur trim), replete with chrome rivets and studs, chains, heavy as hell…… my thoughts drifted to Philip and……

CHAPTER 2
Vocation Conscription

"Oh Mom, come on' do I really have to go?"

"Glint, you're coming with me to Aunt Nancy's house for a visit, and that's that!"

"What about Philip—can't he go? I always go! He never goes! It's his turn!

Damn—nothing was working. I'm screwed!

I apparently was given the name, Glint, in honor of some look that allegedly occurred in my father's eye around the time of my conception. At least that's what my brother, Philip, always told me (particularly whenever I had cleverly offered an 'I love you mom and dad card' at an opportune moment).

I thought, 'Great—another afternoon shot. At least she'll have those good Italian cookies—annesette toast by Stella something—Stella D'Oro I think.' They were great to dunk, but there was a critical window of removal time, which, if exceeded, would result in the end of the long, crescent shaped cookie plopping back into the milk. This would necessitate fishing it out with your fingers—not an easy task. Nonetheless, the cookies offered little solace for a 7 year-old who would rather be out in the "lots" with his friends. (The lots were a large, undeveloped area with woods, open areas, some really big boulders, and many sticks [well suited for adoption as guns, swords, staffs, or other weapons]).

Aunt Nancy's house stood on a hill overlooking the only street in town that had an island of grass running down the center that was to be avoided at all costs because of the curse of heavy dog traffic. It was cleverly named Boulevard Avenue (those town fathers were damn creative in their prime). As I remember it, it seemed like you had to go up at least a hundred steps that were at a 65 degree angle to get to Aunt Nancy's front door. I always refused to look back—terrified that I would fall down the mother of all flights of stairs, only to have my battered body bounce and land on the grass median of Boulevard Avenue, right smack in something left by a Great Dane, to then be mowed over by the town public works guys (whom I vividly remember as having few, if any, teeth, dirty, sleeveless t-shirts, and skinny, stinky cigars that looked like petrified licorice----fondly called *guinea rolls* by the non-appreciative masses—actually, come to think of it, the athletic t-shirts were called *guinea tee's* too).

"By the way, Glint, you really need to behave—Father McMonty is coming for tea today."

Father McMonty was a kindly soul. He always liked to entertain the kids of the parish with tricks, riddles, and small trinkets. He was like the Pied Piper of Fairview. Although his interest in the youngsters might be viewed warily by contemporary parents, everyone accepted his behavior, and I believe that his intentions were genuine and beyond reproach. That's not to say that anything would happen if they weren't. Hell, if a priest told any of our parents we were possessed or we were vampires or something, they would, without question, dutifully run a stake through our heart, convene an exorcism, douse us with holy water in a Catholic form of waterboarding, stuff us with garlic, or other similar actions—all the while trancelike, saying the rosary and bowing to the priest who absolutely was never, never, ever wrong and possessing the knowledge of everything from the experiences of purgatory to small engine repair.

Speaking of saying rosaries, it was a splendid pastime enjoyed by at least half the town, and quite intriguing to the casual observer. Little old ladies, dressed in black, holding a string of black beads, strategically placed between the thumb and forefinger—we clandestinely referred to them as *The Ladies in Black*!!! These ladies adroitly moved their fingers along the beads over and over with mind boggling speed and dexterity— eyes half closed and sometimes rolling up in their heads, saliva caking in the corners of their mouths as they whispered stuff. They were hypnotized or something, sort of like in a trance. If you watched them long enough, you'd get hypnotized yourself and maybe even drool— that's why I would keep one eye closed and only looked at them for a few seconds at a time, lest I, too, fall under the spell. I often had the urge to sneak up behind them and scream something with a make-believe Italian accent —like, 'Fire!!' or 'There's the Pope!' or some other creative attention-getter, just to see if they really were in a trance. I heard that the more rosaries you say, the less time you'd have to spend in Purgatory before you would move up to heaven. These LIB (clever acronym for Ladies in Black—first inkling of a possible career in academics) were, without doubt, well ahead of the game. With their amassed rosary mother lode, they probably only had to spend a total duration of 46 seconds in purgatory before going right up to the pearly gates to shake hands with St. Peter. Just like a Catholic Monopoly game—pass Go, collect twelve dispensations. I wondered if they could have some kind of loan fund for those less adept at power rosary techniques.

I remember a neighbor, Willie, who, later, when I reached the age of 16, used to drive me to my summer job at the pen factory. For some reason, Willie hated people saying the rosary—rosariodysphobia, I bet. Riding along with Willie and me was this lady, Sorella. Sorella had blond hair and wore it in a bun (Connie reminds me of her), always dressed totally in black (replete with a black shawl), and *constantly* whispered the rosary. The blond hair and numerous, pearly teeth distinguished her from the more traditional, hardcore LIB's. Nonetheless, this behavior made it difficult to converse, because she either had long delays in responding (until she finished the particular Hail Mary or some other prayer that she was whispering), needed you to repeat the question, or simply ignored you altogether.

"Hello Sorella."

"Mumble, mumble, mea culpa."

"How are you today?"

"Sssss, ssssss, mumble, mea maxima culpa."

"What do you think of those Yankees?!"

"Mumble, sssss, culpa, culpa."

I think she liked the Yankees, but I suspect she expressed this fondness in some type of Italian code.

I never did figure out why she wore black. Her husband didn't die or anything because she was never married. Willie, in a demonstration of his crisp wit, used to say that her dog died (I don't think she had a dog either)—I always thought she was part nun. Regardless, Willie often kept himself amused on those drives, (and me too I might add) at poor Sorella's expense. With a covert, wry grin while peering out the right corners of his eyes he suddenly would hit the brakes and watch Sorella open her eyes while bolting forward up and out of her seat and coming precariously close to the windshield, a bloody impact averted by Sorella dropping her rosary and simultaneously giving the dash two straight-arms (we didn't have seat belts in those days—or at least Willie didn't have them—I recall that he later said if the car ever crashed and caught on fire you would be stuck and roast to a crisp if you wore your seat belt). The apply-the-brakes-suddenly maneuver was promptly followed by a frenzy of kissing-the-crucifix of the rosary that was retrieved from the floor, and Willie trying to restrain himself from howling and maybe even wetting his pants. Willie did turn pretty red, though, and sometimes he turned to look out the driver's side window to avoid looking at Sorella. During these episodes, I was typically retrieving my lunch bag from the floor of the back seat, but could see his contorted facial expressions in the rearview mirror. I think assembling pens day after day for many years affected Willie's mind. I personally believe that Willie would have cried profusely if Sorella actually had messed up his interior by hitting the windshield. He *loved* that 1961 green Plymouth Fury. Willie always proudly stated that he never had to add "erl" (aka oil) between scheduled changes—although I often wondered about his brake fluid. I think that one of Willie's hobbies was "erl changing" second only to *waushin'* the noble, green chariot. Willie was easily amused.

Back to Father McMonty. He always had an extra rosary that he gave away to the kid who could answer the religion questions of the day. I think Bobby Mantoni must have had a shoebox full, although when queried, he always vehemently denied bartering or selling them to the Ladies in Black. I was skeptical, nonetheless. No matter how hard I tried to answer Father McMonty's question, my answer would either be too late or really, really wrong.

"So is missing a holy day of obligation (I had no idea what that was, except it sounded important) a mortal or a venial sin?" queried Father McMonty.

"I think it's...." I stammered as I was trying to conjure up an answer as quickly as possible plus I had a 50/50 chance of being right.

"A MORTAL SIN!" exclaimed Bobby.

"That's correct Bobby, now what does 'et cum spiritu tuo' mean?"

"You can bring your spirit too!" I proudly blurted, well ahead of Bobby.

The look on Father McMonty's face was one of confusion, at least initially—being perceptive, I quickly realized I had screwed up again and may have a few additional days added to my future stint in purgatory. I felt like this was the Catholic Gong Show!!! And I was always getting the gong! Bobby subsequently answered that one right and once again received the coveted prize—yes, again!

Bobby should have been on Jeopardy on High or something.

I often was confused why Father McMonty would visit Aunt Nancy. She regularly attended Our Lady of the Most Highest Extreme Holiness and Grace Church, but Father McMonty came from St. John the Immaculate Saint of All Saints in Heaven Church— the former was ethnic Italian, the latter, steadfastly Irish. I, being of mixed ethnic pedigree, theoretically could attend either. But Aunt Nancy was as Italian as lasagna. I guess being a priest transcends ethnicity, although I'm sure Father McMonty was clueless when the ladies in black jabbered amongst themselves. I think he assumed it was a Latin dialect.

We went into Aunt Nancy's foyer and I immediately heard the coo-koo clock. For some reason I hated the damn thing. My mother insisted it was imported from Switzerland, which I think was close to Hoboken. I figured it was a plot—the Swiss (wherever they were) simply wanted to get rid of the stupid things and shipped them to Hoboken. Besides the cookoo sound, there always was a musty smell. It could have been the plastic, I guess. Every piece of living room furniture was snugly covered in the shiny, clear film to protect it and make it look like new for at least twenty or thirty years. However, while effectively reducing any wear and tear, this made sitting on the furniture a particularly tricky task in the summertime, particularly because Aunt Nancy didn't have air conditioning—said it made her nose stuffy. (I would later learn to call this rationalization). One had to hold on tightly to the arms of the furniture, lest the unwitting visitor slip like a greased rocket right off the slick surface. It was definitely worse on hot days. You were particularly doomed if you had to sit in the middle. One time I did have to sit in the middle of the sofa (on a very hot day), lost my grip, propelled forward like I was on a waterslide ride, and flopped flat on my back at the foot of the ladies in black—staring straight up Mrs. Stanzone's dress. That was very scary—a PTSD-inducing experience without doubt! To my bewilderment (and consternation), my mother wouldn't believe it was an accident. She refused to believe that the *last* thing I would have wanted was a gander at Mrs. Stanzone's underwear!

Aunt Nancy greeted us and did her fabled grab-and-tweak-your-left-cheek-until-you-almost-fainted routine. I think that is why to this day my face seems asymmetrical when I gaze into the mirror. Maybe it caused Bell's palsy or something—maybe even contra coup! The vigorous, rapid back and forth tugging (she was famously accomplished in this technique) often caused a vacuum and a squishing sound in my mouth. Aunt Nancy was also a bona fide, card-carrying *Lady in Black*, complete with black stockings and rosary. She had a round body, placed atop two rather short, spindly, bowed legs. She usually wore a sweater—I think she had the world's largest collection of sweaters—unfortunately,

99% of them were black. Had I known about ninjas back then, I would have suspected she was some sort of Grand Dame of ninjahood. A secret splinter cell of the LIB!!

Aunt Nancy was *always* very happy. Looking back, I wonder if that had anything to do with Uncle Louie's legendary grappa works in the basement. (I later learned that grappa was a high octane gazillion proof wine that was made from the leftovers of the first round of wine making—guaranteed to leave one's tongue and teeth with a purple hue for weeks on end). I hardly remember Uncle Louie, as he died when I was a baby. I liked to mention his name though, because every time I did Aunt Nancy launched into a make-the-sign-of-the-cross-kiss-the-rosary frenzy with additional, assorted mutterings and gestures. I once said Uncle Louie's name NINE times in a row. Each time it was followed by that thoroughly amazing, breath-taking ritual! Great fun, particularly since Aunt Nancy was babysitting me and mom wasn't around to thump me on the back of the head.

The late Uncle Louie made a special brand of near-lethal wine from the residue of less lethal wine and had barrels stored everywhere in the basement. A never-ending supply I assumed, but I never verified that fact, because I was terrified to go down to the cellar. Never went down there, lest the monster from behind the barrels get me! Not to mention that Dracula, Wolfman, the Mummy, Frankenstein, zombies, and maybe even the ghost of UNCLE LOUIE could be lurking down there! The ambience was enhanced by the fact that there was one light bulb with a string situated smack in the center of the cellar. Philip told me that you had to grope around in the dark to find it, not knowing what else you might touch in the meantime. That didn't seem to deter Aunt Nancy, though. They also had a cat down there whose sole mission in life was to catch mice in the dark. It rarely came up to daylight, so I wasn't sure if it was part mole or if it could even see!

We sat down in the dining room, (with no plastic on the chairs except for the cushions), and had the usual priest-comes-for-tea discussions. Suddenly, as if on cue, Father McMonty would bolt out of his seat, stare up at the ceiling (I looked up there on numerous occasions, but didn't see anything), slowly close his eyes and say, "I have a special feeling that someone in this room is going to become a priest!" I think he actually said "premonition" but I didn't know what that meant at the time, guessing it was very important, and something the Pope would do.

Now I might have been young, but I didn't just fall off the pumpkin truck! No siree! There were exactly *four* people in the room; Father McMonty, Aunt Nancy, my mother, and me. Father McMonty *already was* a priest. Aunt Nancy was too old, a full fledged member of the Ladies in Black and a *girl* (albeit an old girl)—and priests are guys. Mom had two strikes against her: 1) she was married (and a *girl* too), and 2) she had kids, both of which absolutely dashed any aspirations for clergyhood. Although I searched the room for another potential candidate the search was in vain---- there was only one, logical possibility. ME! Hell I was desperate—almost to the point of dashing to the basement, and throwing myself to the mercy of monsters or even Uncle Louie's ghost! Once this declaration was uttered by Father McMonty, six eyeballs zoomed in me, the gazes going right through my skull like lasers. Male, no kids, not married, altar boy, Irish *and* Italian—damn I had all the tickets –no, a FULL-HOUSE (even if I was a dunce in Father Mc Monty's Catholic Jeopardy Q & A game)! It was ME! Where was Bobby when I needed him!? I was GOING TO BE A PRIEST—and wear black clothes, and drink wine on the altar, and ask Catholic questions, and learn Latin, and bless everybody, and put ashes on people's foreheads and be celibate (I thought that was like being Polish). Ye gads!!!

By the time I realized I was the candidate, three mouths broadened into smiles—mine puckered as if lemons and Crazy Glue had been poured into it. Then the gaze of the three adults slowly drifted toward the ceiling (again I still couldn't see anything up there) eyes closed, and their hands came together in silent prayer. In those days, becoming a priest was like becoming the President or winning the Medal of Honor, or becoming a candidate in line to be the next Pope—I think every family wanted to have someone in the running. That's probably why families were bigger then (part of the Catholic thing)—they always had a stable of eligible males for priestly duties, but kept some others in reserve to maintain the family name. I, even at the ripe age of 9, had other ideas, inspired by the graphic renditions of Lou Ferrara's love conquests, overheard in the alley. Even though I had no idea what he was talking about at the time, I knew I would like girls some day, although for the life of me at this point I couldn't figure out why.

I feigned a smile that caused Aunt Nancy and my mother to both gleefully launch into a maniacal, ruthless, "tweak-your-cheek-you-good-boy" frenzy. They did it in unison—one on each side, as if choreographed to a 33 1/3 rpm polka, played at 78. I thought they were on the verge of ripping my cheeks off or at least making me permanently look like a hamster with sagging jowls. Out of desperation, I almost yelled out, "Uncle Louie" just to sidetrack Aunt Nancy into releasing her tenacious grip and launch into a sign-of-the-cross diversion. Unfortunately, the cheek stretching made it virtually impossible to move my lips in any useful fashion—the only sound I could make was something like 'urrg-ghhh.' Through squinting, tearful eyes I peered over to Father McMonty who was contentedly dunking cookies into his tea. *MY COOKIES*!!! Talk about adding insult to injury! Here I was, having my face systematically disfigured (in stereo) with new dimples being sculpted manually and without anesthesia, all while the coveted reward for visiting Aunt Nancy was disappearing right before my tearful, squinting, and now rapidly widening eyes!

Finally, with fatigue draining the vice-like grips of their thumbs and index fingers, I was able to wiggle free from Mom and Aunt Nancy, my face frozen into a wide, Alfred E. Neuman, 'what-me worry?' grin—this prompting the ladies to say, "See how happy he is! He's *so* proud and excited about becoming a priest!—he can't wait!"

"Arrrrggggghhhhh," I gurgled, still unable to move my mouth that was frozen in a Jack-O-Lantern grimace. I suddenly realized that I couldn't chew cookies even if, by chance, there were any left! Then again, with the added cheek volume, perhaps I could have stored the cookies for later consumption—sort of like a hamster.

Mom, Aunt Nancy and Father McMonty all sat and had tea, chatting about life in the seminary. For the longest time, I thought that's where dead people were.

The events of the grueling afternoon were drawing to a close. Mom took my hand and led me down the flight of the zillion steps. If I fell now, at least they would find a smile on my bruised and battered body as it reposed on the dog-defiled, grassy median.

'He was a nice boy—smiled to the very end—probably overwhelmed about the prospect of becoming a member of the clergy. Stomach contents empty— no cookies found.'

We bid goodbye and I took solace in the fact that at least Father McMonty didn't say that someone was going to be the next *Bishop* (nor did he give specific time lines for the priest part)! We strolled home, my mother and I both smiling—albeit for different reasons. Feeling was slowly returning to my face.

"Say Mom, y'know Philip told me *he* wants to be a priest, but I'm not supposed to tell anyone-it's a secret." I had my fingers crossed in my right pants pocket, so that prevented me from losing any rosary bonuses that I might have already accrued, due to lying . Besides it was a little lie, therefore falling into the category of a venial sin which usually allowed for time off for good behavior or maybe probation.

"Oh, really? Maybe he should come see Father McMonty the next time!"

Now my smile was genuine.

CHAPTER 3
Next Session: The Collector

"Mr. and Mrs. Tunnoose are here Dr. Wayward," Connie warbled over the intercom.

"Well, hello Mr. and Mrs. Tunnoose, how have you been?"

"Been better," said Mrs. Tunnoose in a sour fashion.

"Things are fine," retorted the spouse.

"If they're so *fine* then why are we here?" she snapped.

"*You* say *I* have a problem. *I* don't think *I* have a problem. That's why," muttered Mr. Tunnoose.

Charming couple, the Tunnooses. Rudolph, (aka Rudy) a tall, lanky, balding man with a prominent nose and sunken, dark-ringed eyes. Luella, a small, petite, minus 2 size woman with poofy reddish hair. He, a man with peculiar tastes. She, a woman who constantly 'reminded' him of the absurdity of his peculiarities, lest he forget. They reminded me of a Mutt and Jeff combination of sorts. I typically was cast into the role of referee in these family sessions.

"So, Mr. Tunnoose, how has your collection issue been going?" I asked in anxious anticipation.

"Go ahead and tell the doctor, Rudy," chirped Mrs.Tunnoose.

"Quit pushing me, Ella!"

"A grown man, collecting those silly things….."

"They're *NOT* silly!"

"A forty year-old man with stuffed animals! *That's* not silly?"

"They're not *just* stuffed animals!"

"No then what in the hell *ARE* they? —I'll tell you what they are…."

"They're *BEANIE BABIES!*" exclaimed Mr. Tunnoose.

"Beanie babies, schmeenie babies! You're embarrassing me. You're embarrassing the *children!* The neighbors think we're fruitcakes! You're wrecking your LIFE!—You're wrecking everybody's life!"

"It's a hobby."

"A grown man—going to *doll shows!* Tell Dr. Wayward how much you spent on *Tessie!*"

"Bessie."

"Tessie, Bessie, who gives a shit! Tell him how much you spent!"

"Forty-five dollars."

"Forty-five dollars for a God-damn *bean bag cow*! Is he *NUTS* or what, doc?"

"Er, I don't call people 'nuts,'" I stated, with a sense of relief that it didn't cost more.

"He's nuts. 100%, certified, shell-on, bona-fide *NUTS!* Like there's some kinda' need for this junk!"

"I'm not nuts—it's a *hobby!*" Mr. Tunnoose reaffirmed weakly.

"Doc, he spends half the day looking through want ads in the Shopper, or on E-Bay or Craigslist searching for the damn things. He looks on-line from his phone—he aimlessly wanders around garage sales. He dumped my books out of the bookcase and has those stupid things all lined up. He even bought more bookcases—that don't even match. He knows all their names. He writes lists of their names. Ever sit watching TV with *HUNDREDS* of pairs of these little, beady eyes staring at you? Nobody even collects the damn things anymore!"

"They don't stare," Mr. Tunnoose replied both meekly and unconvincingly.

"He puts them up there. He takes them down. He moves one here. He moves one there. He *talks* to them! He even has to have them sit in a certain way and in particular order!"

"That's not totally true. She's making that up," responded Rudolph, less meekly but even more unconvincingly.

"That's not *TRUE*!?!? Making it up!?! Ask your kids! Ask your poor 80 year-old mother who doesn't even like to come over anymore! She thinks her son is a wuss! Hell she flat out says you're odd!"

"Mom doesn't think that—she doesn't even know what 'wuss' means….She gets mean," he said, nodding his head toward Mrs. Tunnoose.

"Gets, mean? How?" I interrupted in an awkward attempt to get into the discussion.

"I *know* she moves the Beanie Babies out of order—maybe even hides some—and on purpose!"

"See, I *told* you Doc!" quipped Mrs. Tunnoose in triumphant, un-bridled glee.

"So, Mr. Tunnoose, your wife seems to think that this hobby is getting the best of you. Perhaps a bit too much, maybe? What do you think?" I said in the most gentle, neutral manner that I could garner up at the time (despite my mounting certainty that OCD was somewhere in the mix).

"Nahhh."

"Well then why does Mrs. Tunnoose think so?" I queried.

"Probably because I'm too busy and I don't pay attention to her," he retorted in a rather wimpy manner.

This left the door wide open for Mrs. T and she hit it with the force of a runaway locomotive. "He checks on the damn things first thing in the morning. He checks when he comes home for lunch. He checks them after dinner. He gets up during the night to check on them. I saw him in there with a flashlight last night!"

"Is that true Mr. Tunnoose?" I asked, leery of the anticipated, forthcoming answer.

"I thought I heard a mouse."

'Definitely unconvincing! Definite downward spiral on the proverbial chart of convincingness. A nadir!'

It slowly became apparent that Mr. Tunnoose had more than a passing fancy with Beanie Babies. He was OBSESSED with them! He had a compulsion to buy as many as he could, whenever he could. The magnitude of the problem was monumental. Mr. T. has been known to stand in long lines typically populated by grandmother-types and young children; to stand in lines snaking through malls, mini-malls, garage sales, and other locations where these treasures could still be found. Lonely vigils and an insatiable quest to obtain the prize of all prizes—the elusive, limited edition Beanie Baby! He maintained a veritable zoo of stuffed animals. A modern-day, renaissance pachydermist. Not to mention his endless hours on E-bay and Craigslist! Personally (and therapists aren't supposed to get personal), the thought of a 6'4" man carrying a suitcase of stuffed lambs, kittens, dogs, cows, crabs and the like, was striking. (Not to mention that there was not a single, practical use that I could identify for them). This underscores the true genius of the inventor— invent something useless, limit the releases, create planned scarcity, come up with clever names, and support an underground network! Poor Mr. T—a hollow shell of his old self! It was almost as tragic as the pro football linebacker whom I treated about 10 years ago. That poor soul was obsessed with Cabbage Patch Kids—another contrived need and cleverly marketed ploy. Funny thing, though----they at least sort of looked like him.

Diagnosis? Good question. Have to call him something. Otherwise the insurance won't pay and Mr. Tunnose will get stiffed—or worse, I'd get the big denial of payment letter from them. How do you explain to a managed care company that your client has an obsession with *Beanie Babies*? Well OCD probably fits the bill—or some type of impulse disorder, or maybe even both.

"Mr. Tunnoose, have you complied with our contract?"

"Sort of."

"Sort of?"

"I only bought 23 this week."

A quick mental calculation—23 x $10.00=$230.00 (at minimum). Probably close to double that if he was at the mercy of sociopathic, sadistic sellers who prey on the Rudy's of the world. Those Beanie Baby scalpers are ruthless and without a conscience! Maybe even without an iota of a conscience!

"Twenty-three more of the damn things!" croaked Mrs. Tunnoose.

"*Only* twenty-three!" Mr. T. responded.

"That's good Mr. Tunnoose. You've continued to reduce your purchases, as planned."

"Yup, and I only traded and sold a few."

"Okay, so now our goal is to reduce the number further. Right?" I asked imploringly.

"I don't want any more of the damn things in my house!" screamed Mrs. Tunnoose. "I want the ones already there out too! Friggin' zoo! Pronto, mister!"

"Now, Mrs. Tunnoose, this has to be a gradual process—we call it successive approximations (It's often helpful to toss in a technical term or two when attempting to sound smart)." Turning to Mr. Tunnoose I asked, "Have you not counted them at lunch time?"

"Yeah, I gave that up. It took too much time—got back to work too late. It's *her* fault about that too. I used to get half way into counting them and then she'd start yelling different numbers out loud. She knew I'd have to start over."

Oniomania is the need to buy things. What in the hell is the need to buy Beanie Babies called? Beanieoniomania? Where the heck would I find that diagnostic code? Poor Mr. Tunnoose—a victim of mass marketing. Funny thing, though, it's a very subtle process. In their heyday I never saw a TV commercial on them, or a billboard, or a newspaper insert. Maybe they use subliminal techniques—slipped in while unsuspecting victims are watching Wheel of Fortune or Gilligan's Island reruns. Or even the shopping channel. Just whispers in the night-"Psst—got Rover?" "Yeah, but what about Whiskers?" "I'll trade a Twigs." An entire, seamy, underworld culture—a black market for Beanie Babies—that hapless victims such as Mr. Tunnoose fall prey to. Many to finally be debased and cast off, ultimately ending up plying their trade in illicit beanie houses! Or pandering them on the street.

"Well, Mr. Tunnoose, we're making progress. Remember you can overcome this problem. Keep sticking to the program and don't buy, sell, or trade to excess.—When the urge comes to buy more—think happy thoughts instead!"

Unfortunately, I knew what his happy thoughts would consist of and it wasn't pretty.

"Okay Doc, see you next week."

Mr. and Mrs Tunnoose got up and strolled out together, hand in hand. As they walked toward the door, I noticed bulges on both of Mr. Tunnoose's hips—right about where the pockets of his checkered sport jacket were located. Could he....?

The door closed and I recorded a few progress notes.

A knock on the door interrupted me. In stepped Connie with a beaming smile and a greyish, sort of tie-dyed, floppy thing clutched in her hand.

"It's Claude the Crab!" she exclaimed, "Isn't he sooo cute? Mr. Tunnoose just sold him to me for 18 dollars—said he had a few extra!"

"Please sit down, Connie....."

Speaking of obsessive-compulsive individuals....

CHAPTER 4
Cousin Joey

"**Glint, help your** mom straighten the living room. Pick up the toys. Philip, put the garbage out—we got to go."

"Okay Dad," I muttered. Another Christmas day, the Waywards on the verge of another traditional trip to Aunt Chris' and Uncle Joe's—and, delight of delights, to see *and* socially interact with cousin Joey. For as long as I could remember, every Christmas merited a journey to Chris and Joe's. For as long as I could remember also, Joey Jr. was a twerp. Only difference was that each year he grew to be an even bigger twerp. Philip thought so too. In fact, that was one of the few things we actually agreed on.

I typically attempted to play with my Christmas gifts to the latest possible second before the over-hyped, inevitable departure. I used to smuggle a toy or two with me, but the old man caught on and now we had to go through a frisking procedure before we left. I found out later he was alerted to the intent to smuggle by my putting my coat on 30 minutes before we were supposed to leave, and the coat appearing overly bulky. Hell, I was young—a few more years of practice and I could have smuggled a bazooka.

We all piled into the spiffy, so-called 'classic' '53 Ford. I was embarrassed to ride in the thing—it always seemed as if pedestrians were trying to peer into the windows to see who could *possibly* be driving around in that tank. We were like the Beverly Hillbillies! It was rusted, needed a muffler, was missing two hubcaps and laid down a smoke cloud that could conceal a bus. Obviously, it burned 'erl.' The vehicle even had this pointed nose with a chrome bullet and a huge visor over the top of the windshield. It was green too; come to think of it, seems like all the cars on Lincoln Street were green like Willie's. Not easy to blend into traffic with that chariot, despite the green color. I affectionately referred to the car as the Batmobile—a brilliant idea, gleaned from D.C. comics. Dad would fire up the bat turbines, use the manual shift on the column, and with a deep-throated chugging (like a lawn mower on steroids) we zoomed off on our merry way—our trail easily identified by the black clouds behind us.

"Jingle bells, jingle bells, jingle all..." Philip and I belted out with glee.

"Shaddap!!!!

Fleeting Christmas spirit.

About half way there, Mom would launch into her traditional, yuletide, be-good-to-Joey litany. *Don't* make fun of him, *don't* put odd things in his food, *don't* go in his room, *don't* call him a twerp, and *don't* play with his new toys unless he says it's okay (not likely). Mom could have saved time by telling us what we *could* do.

Aunt Chris and Uncle Joe lived about 30 minutes away, depending on whether Dad got lost or not. He often did, which was a constant source of amusement. We typically became suspicious about his sense of direction when we passed Charlie's Deli more than once during the first leg of the trip. If we passed it more than three times on the first leg of the journey, we were *really* screwed. This situation was even more mystifying because Mom gave him directions and she has never driven a car (never even bothered to get a driver's license). Assuming it was a good day and we were correctly headed west, sooner or later, we'd get to the *meadowlands!* And in the meadowlands was *OVERPECK CREEK!!*-a frothy, choppy, murky expanse of COLD water. And spanning Overpeck Creek was….*the bridge from hell*! It wasn't a big bridge, but it was really narrow and close to the water. I actually had dreams about water crashing over the sides and washing the Batmobile into the perilous creek —which I *knew* had to be at least 1000 feet deep at its shallowest point and with really big fish with really big teeth lurking below. It was always windy to boot…again adding to the vision of us being blown off the bridge into the choppy water with who knows what prowling underneath. I wondered just how watertight the Batmobile was, but that hole in the floorboard below Mom's feet (cleverly hidden by a piece of plywood and a rubber mat that the old man found somewhere) wasn't very reassuring. In other words, it was the friggin' Titanic with holes like a huge swiss cheese!

The return trip was traditionally more hair-raising. The approach to the bridge was downhill, with a mean 90-degree right-hand turn. The Cyclone roller coaster at Palisades' Amusement Park paled in comparison. If dad didn't make that turn it was swim city—and I couldn't swim! It was curtains! I periodically would entertain the possibility of bringing water wings or an inflatable tube along on the Christmas pilgrimage. I'm sure Dad would have found that peculiar, him being an ex-sailor and everything. Besides, he might take that as a personal affront to his driving prowess and those life-saving buoyant devices were somewhere in our cellar. So my fate was in the hands of the river gods (with a little help from one of Bobby's stash of answer-Father McMonty's question-and-win-a-rosary, rosaries). I even opted for baggy clothing, hoping that in the event of a disaster, the arms and legs would fill up with air allowing me to slowly drift to safety.

Ye gads. Careening off —airborne into Overpeck Creek. Slicing through the gargantuan whitecaps! Philip and I screaming our heads off—Mom closing her eyes fumbling for her rosary (and hopefully keeping enough foot pressure on the plywood floor repair to keep water from gushing in)—Dad singing row-row-row-the-boat...

"Glint?"

Whoops, back to reality. "Yes Dad?"

"Rub that back window! It's too damn foggy."

Arrggghhh. One more thing to seal our doom! The trip became particularly dicey when there was snow on the ground. I employed various stress-reduction tactics—closing my eyes, holding my breath (got too dizzy with that one; plus I could only go a few blocks), and even visualizing the Ladies in Black casting their hypnotic spell. All to no avail. Of course Philip would capitalize on the occasion by telling me about the mutant, prehistoric catfish from hell (aka BIG SLIPPERY) that lurked in the bottom of that despicable creek, just waiting to dine on unsuspecting Christmas pilgrims as they slowly sank to the bottom! Or, if Philip was feeling particularly sadistic (like after I broke his new Robert the Robot Christmas present eight minutes after he opened it), he might make his famous squealing tire sounds, or just simply scream, "We're gonna die!" (that usually earned him a backhand from Dad—I'm still amazed at the distance Dad could cover with his right arm (without even looking!)—hell if he was pissed enough he could have hit us even if we were sitting in the trunk!).

When we arrived at Chris and Joe's, Joey would typically be up in his room, resting or something. He rested a lot. At least these relatives didn't launch into a tweek-your-cheek treatment…only part Italian I think. Dad made a beeline to the refrigerator and popped open a cold one— one in a long line for the evening. He also was less than thrilled about this annual adventure, and his way of dealing with it was simple—he got bombed. He was much happier then. I kept a silent count of number of cans consumed. Fancying myself as a junior scientist, I was certain that there was a positive relationship between the number of cans consumed, Dad's level of cheerfulness, and the increased risk of swimming with the catfish. There was an equally compelling relationship between the number of sips of left-over beer that I retrieved from Dad's discarded cans and the reduction of my bridgeophobia.

The Christmas tree was particularly memorable. Aunt Chris and Uncle Joe hung the usual garland around the tree. What made it unique (at least in my limited experience with Christmas trees) was that tinsel was placed, one piece at a time, meticulously, and with the utmost care. The length of each strand was *exactly* the same—the distance between strands was *exactly* the same—the front *and* the back of the tree were *exactly* the same—hell the praises that my parents and Chris and Uncle Joe gave to Joey for his fine job were *exactly* the same. It became *exactly* obvious that Joey had too much free time on his hands.

From a very young age, as a budding psychologist I thought this was a bit peculiar. Actually, more than a bit. So did Philip (a second thing that we agreed on). It must have taken Joey several days to get the presentation just right. It only took Philip and me about 12 seconds to secretly "rearrange" some of the tinsel.

Dad didn't say too much by the time we all sat marveling about the tree, waiting for Joey to make a grand appearance. I think the beer and the fact that he routinely forgot his glasses (another harbinger of the treacherous return ride to come) made the tinsel look like a silver blur of Reynold's Wrap, preventing him from appreciating the true intricacy and preciseness of the work. The way Chris and Joe acted, Joey was going to go to Harvard on a tree-decorating scholarship or something. Maybe make Time Magazine's Conifer Decorator of the Year or design Macy's New York store window Christmas display (that was a big attraction in those days).

Then entered Joey. The adults always acted surprised. Except for Dad. He viewed this as an opportune time to fetch another brewski. The "surprise" factor was particularly baffling, as for the last who knows how many years, the ritual was *exactly* the same. You had to be a box of rocks to actually be surprised! Joey was a pudgy, bespectacled, kid with a flat-top haircut (the front standing straight up with the aid of butch wax), and rather prominent ears. His hair was bright red. Philip and I didn't know the term, dork, at that time. If we did, Joey definitely would have been identified as one. To top it off, he had a lisp. We exchanged the routine pleasantries, with Philip and I waiting in anxious anticipation for Joey to notice our tinsel shenanigans. As he stood beaming at the tree, his look of delight gradually transformed (actually sort of melted) into one of terror, punctuated by hints of anguish. His eyes widened, his mouth opened, and he definitely turned pretty darn red. His freckles all seemed to connect together and he let loose with a guttural howl. Philip and I busied ourselves with our new presents that we weren't supposed to know were brought by our parents and covertly placed under the 'tree of meticulousity.' Joey bolted for the tree and dutifully began the tinsel reorganization in earnest. Actually, it was more than in earnest—he was going full throttle in a rather maniacal manner. That kept him busy for quite some time. Joey tended to be easily amused.

This diversion also allowed either Philip or me (depending on whose turn it was that particular year) to sneak off to 'the room at the top of the stairs' (aka Joey's room). It was "off limits" to the Wayward youths. Joey had a zillion stuffed animals all over the place. Shelves, bookcase, window seat, floor, and, of course, the bed was teeming with them! (Never did figure out how he could sleep there). They too were meticulously arranged—simply too tempting. It was my year for the stuffed animal rearrangement campaign and so I dutifully took one from here and put it there, one from there and put it here, hid several under his bed, and placed several others together in unusual positions that I had seen in one of Lou Ferrara's graphic magazines that he hid under his porch. I was clueless as to what those naked people were actually doing, except I saw Rusty the dog do that to Muffy once. Too bad I couldn't watch Joey's reaction. One year we lucked out and did hear him howl when he went up there, but we were in the process of the quest home and scampered to the Batmobile.

Joey also had other quirks (aka flat-out weird behaviors). He called his parents by their first names. Chris was a nurse and she read somewhere that this was now the proper, new way to raise children. I tried that once myself at home—unfortunately, that excursion into name familiarity earned me a round of slap therapy from my father. Unbeknownst to me at the time, Dad had a *definite* preference for being called 'Dad.' Period. Okay, maybe Pop was okay too but that was the absolute limit. Joey's parent beckoning was made all the more interesting by his articulation problem which resulted in "Kwis and Wosuph." Philip and I thought this was a definite knee-slapper, prompting us to have Joey repeat things like, "the red ranger rode really roughly."

"The wed wanger wode weally wuffly."

"Hee, hee, hee." 'he's just like Elmer Fudd!', we mused.

"Kwis and Wosuph----thewyre doing it again!"

Dinner was another priceless, time-honored tradition. Everyone had a place setting except Joey. He had a Howdy Doody plastic plate and drank from some kind of straw that was twisted into a million turns. He liked to watch the milk race through it. Again, Joey was easily amused. The Waywards sat on one side facing Aunt Chris, Joey, and Wosuph, er— Uncle Joe, who sat on the other side. Philip and I were finicky eaters, but Joey was the finickmeister. We ate ham—he ate macaroni and cheese. We protested but ate sweet potatoes—he ate macaroni and cheese. We gagged on green bean salad—he ate applesauce. Chris had read that kids eat when they're hungry and they know when their body is missing some vital nutrient and then they eat food or other objects that contain it. Mom, always the skeptic, didn't buy that one…so much for my twinkie pica. Joey would disappear from the table periodically, only to return for another bite of macaroni and cheese. I think he would covertly do a spot check on the Christmas tree tinsel. It was during these times, when Mom and Aunt Chris would be clearing off the table and Dad and Uncle Joe would go watch TV (and Joey off spot-checking) that Philip and I could put things in Joey's applesauce or his Mac & Cheese. Salt, sugar, pepper, lint, or any other easily concealed condiment fit the bill. We only got caught once—I overzealously, and with reckless abandon put a marble in his macaroni and cheese. He almost swallowed it but at the last gag spit it onto his Howdy Doody dish where it clacked around in circles. Everyone was perplexed and Uncle Joe insisted that he would write the Kraft Mac & Cheese company the very next day, enclosing the marble as evidence. The meal would go on for hours at least. I was glad to see the pecan pie roll out, as this was a signal that it was soon time to face destiny and maybe even make it home to play with our new toys.

We put our presents into the Bat trunk, fired up the turbines and were off—Philip and I straining to hear a howl from upstairs or see a silhouette in the window maniacally bobbing about, waving stuffed objects in its hands.

"Did you do anything nasty to your cousin Joey this time?" Mom would ask.

No response from the back seat.

"Did you two mess up the tree again?"

Muffled giggles from the back seat.

"You better not have gone upstairs again either!" croaked Dad.

Fear in the back seat.

Philip would usually fall asleep—guess he wasn't too worried about the bridge. Mom would usually tell Dad the directions home, interspersing those with a barrage of "slow down's," these often accompanied by eyes closing, some type of "sssss" sound and a head turn to the right Then it was finally the moment of reckoning. We crested the hill and barreled down toward the bridge. Trying to contain the shrieking in my mind I attempted mental telepathy with Dad.

"Right turn. Right turn. Think right turn."

Faster, and faster—the thought of the mother of all catfish waiting below the icy waves—bat turbines whining like crazy-----

"Right turn, right turn, slow down—break out the water wings!!"

I ducked behind the sleeping Philip, both of us behind Mom (I figured the extra weight on the right side may have some benefit). Where's that rosary anyhow?

Then, I felt myself sliding toward the left, heard the drone of the tires on the bridge's metalwork, and *KNEW* we had survived another harrowing, death defying, up- yours passage over Overpeck Creek! Too bad Old

Slippery—we live for another day! Thanks God, but I was only kidding about taking Father McMonty up on his vocation offer.

We arrived home (Dad only passed Charlie's Deli twice) and as the Batmobile slid up to the curb, I gazed over at the peaceful Philip. He had an angelic smile and rested his head ever so gently on a fluffy, white, STUFFED BUNNY! Yes, a STUFFED BUNNY!!! I marveled at how he pulled that caper off—there was definitely a newly found respect for my older brother. Definitely, howling was still going full force, in Bogota, NJ! The image of an agitated silhouette prominent in the upstairs window was vivid in my mind . Ho, ho, ho, Merry Christmas!!

CHAPTER 5
Session 3—Group Therapy

"Okay people, I'd like to begin," I said, clearing my throat. "I think since this is our first session, we need to introduce ourselves and perhaps even mention what you'd like to get out of these group sessions."

This was the first session for my cat-lovers-gone-overboard group, cleverly named the more socially acceptable Feline Pet Lovers Support Group. I sat gazing around the room at the six individuals and mused how managed care had driven me to this zenith of creativity. One step removed from a pet psychologist! It only took three days to fill all the openings in the group, after strategically placing an ad in Shoppers' Showplace (and weeding out dog-lovers gone overboard—the makings of yet another group). I knew there was a multitude of these poor souls out there, trapped in feline-dominated domiciles, reading Shoppers' Showplace to lessen their misery. One of my psychiatrist friends accused me of engaging in a simple pay-the-rent ploy. He said I ran this group just because I could get $50 a head up front—buckos on the barrelhead—without managed care treatment plans, phone calls to accountants-turned-case-managers, paltry fees, or late payments. Imagine that! Considering the situation in that light, maybe I was both *creative* and *pragmatic,* on the verge of launching a new pyramid scheme of mental health!

"How's about we start with you, Mrs. Grobman."

"I'm Irene Grobman," she stated in squeaky, nasal Brooklynese.

Silence.

Attempting to fill the void, I piped up, "Er, Mrs. Grobman, can you tell the group a bit about yourself?"

"Yeah, c'mon toots, let's heah it," boomed Ethel Wiseman.

Ethel was a decorated veteran of a variety of psychotherapy groups –eight I think—rumor had it she was the motivating force for the demise of at least six. I feared she was fast out of the gate toward number seven.

"Now, now Mrs. Wiseman, let's please give Mrs. Grobman a chance."

"Is *everybody* here Jewish?" queried Ida Guiliani.

"I'm Greek, thank you," declared the portly lady to the right, "Maria Kilelacas."

Four down and two to go I thought to myself.

"And who are you two?" demanded Ethel Wiseman in her best Attilla-the-group- therapy-member manner.

"Percy Nottingham," said the rather gaunt, bespectacled, solitary male group member.

"*Poicy!* What kind of a name is *Poicy*?" squawked Ethel.

"Mrs. Wiseman, I think it would be best for you to stop being so confrontational!" I interjected.

"Confrontational my ass! *Poicy*….sounds like a fruitloop…" she muttered at a decibel level just loud enough to be heard..

'Definitely going for group demise number seven.' I thought.

"I'm Lucinda Walker, but you can call me Lucy," said the final member of the merry sextet.

"Mrs. Wiseman, why don't *you* start by telling the group a little about yourself," I said in my best 'hoping to redirect' manner.

"Yeah, okay doc. I'm Ethel Wiseman and I'm here because I need to talk about my cat, Pixie."

She rummaged around and took a photo out of her wallet and passed it around to the assorted "oohhhs" and "aahhhs" of the group. The old polaroid finally made it to me. Pixie was basically a white, fluffy, HUMONGOUS cat with pink-looking eyes. I think it was an albino opossum or something. Without doubt it looked like it could definitely wade through and destroy (with impunity) a slew of 'Muffy the lap dog' types in a matter of seconds.

A feline on illicit, performance-enhancing steroids!

"Pixie-pooh doesn't like me to go out and leave her. If I do, she usually tinkles on the dining room table. I had to put a plastic table cloth on it to protect the wood!" complained Ethel.

'Pixie-*pooh*...' I thought to myself, 'must make for an interesting Christmas dinner at that table. I could see Cousin Joey.....'

"I'm Irene, like I said before," squeaked Mrs. Grobman in a definitively Betty Boopish way. "I have a cat Boopsie ['*Boopsie*, please God give me inner strength,' I secretly pleaded] who simply refuses to eat anything but smoked salmon or chopped filet mignon. The poor thing would starve himself rather than eat *anything* else!"

'Self-limiting disorder,' I thought.

"Boopsie will eat plants and *puke* if I don't give him what he likes," she continued. "I've had to go to the deli during blizzards when we've run out of salmon."

'One less, very *cold*, starved feline in my house,' I thought.

"My cat is very high-strung," volunteered Ms. Guiliani.

'Nice way of saying schizophrenic,' I thought.

"His name is Maxwell, and Maxwell has a *temper!*" she stammered.

'Okay, maybe intermittent explosive disorder—do cats have that?' I thought.

"If you sit in *his* chair he gets really mad. If someone comes to visit he gets mad. If you don't totally clean his litter box...."

"He gets mad!" interjected Mrs. Wiseman, obviously very proud of new-found, keen ability to connect the dots and make a summary statement.

I noticed that Ida Guiliani's hands had scores of red lines all over them, all in various stages of healing. Her hose had series of parallel lines running down—all precisely a claw-width apart. The edge of her dress had several rather tattered sections—another telltale sign of cat owner abuse! Poor woman, brutalized in her own home by a maniacal feline—MAD MAX!

'Old Max is a candidate for an appointment with Mongo the pit bull,' I thought. 'Wonder if Ida ever heard of the term, *declawing*!'

"You *poor thing!*" empathized Maria Kilelacas. "How do you stand it?"

"I *love* the big lug!" Ida wailed, dabbing her eyes with a Kleenex.

"Now, now, love sometimes makes us do things that don't truly fit the criteria for being rational," I stated therapeutically while handing Ida a box of tissues—the one she was using was now the size of a quarter.

Honk.

'What in the hell am I *saying?*' I asked myself.

"I'm allergic to cat hair, but I can't get rid of my cat!" blurted out Maria, also choking back tears.

'Needs a bald cat, or maybe fish as pets' I very cleverly mused to myself in a minimally empathic manner.

"My doctor said it's either have asthma or get rid of the cat—but Bootsie is a member of the *family*! See…" she said as she too distributed a picture for group inspection—a 5 by 7 to boot!

'Pixie, Boopsie, Bootsie— does every cat have an 'ie' at the end of its name? Maybe even Maxie!' I thought.

Again, a chorus of "ahhhs" and "ooohs."

'Sure as hell looks like a typical cat to me,' I thought, 'one of those calico numbers.' I smiled in an attempt to conceal my rapidly developing cat contempt.

"So how do you handle it?" asked Percy.

"Every day I take Zyrtec, and Sudafed, and Vaconase, and Vitamin C, and St.John's Wort, and Ginseng, and Ginkobiloba, and nose drops. I also buy those surgical masks like they wear in China. I give Bootsie a bath every week too," she replied.

'At least she doesn't have scratches, must have used the declawing option' I mused.

"Good thing I had him declawed and neutered…makes it easier to wash him," said Maria.

'Now she's thinking!—must have read her mind!' I cheered to myself.

Miss Walker's turn.

"My cat's only problem is that he claws all the furniture—not me—just everything else!" said Lucy.

'Another candidate for claw-plucking,' I thought.

"I keep spraying that cat-away stuff over everything, but it doesn't work. I have to put plastic seat covers all over my house—that *bad* Ravel!"

'At least it's not *Ravellie*! Must be a bitch sitting on the couch in the summer,'

I reflected, reminiscing about Aunt Nancy's abode.

"I put boxes and pieces of cardboard and pieces of old rugs on the table legs, arms of the furniture, and any other exposed parts—that bad Ravellie still finds a way to scratch them!" she continued.

'Ravellie—aaarrrggghhh!'

"Maybe Ravellie—er, Ravel is an outdoor cat by nature," I stated, thinking that at the very least he *certainly* should start to be!

"I just can't let him go through the pain of having his claws removed!" Lucy choked out.

'Less painful than a beheading,' I mused to myself.

"My house looks like it's *totally* tattered!" she continued.

"More like Sanford and Son's,' I thought. 'Can't do much therapeutic work here unless I convince her that declawing is less painful than a beheading' I mused to myself.

Finally it was Percy Nottingham's turn.

"Actually, Mr. Peepers is well behaved. It's my neighbors who are causing problems. They keep urging the owner and landlord to change the apartment building to a 'no pet' status condo. They say she howls.

"You did say *Mr.* Peepers didn't you?" queried Ethel.

"Ambiguous genitalia when she was a kitten," Percy replied.

'Don't touch that one,' I cautioned myself.

"The neighbors also make fun of me when I take Mr. Peepers for walks. I *do* keep her on a leash and make her use the gutter. They even laugh at me when I drive her around in my Volkswagon beetle. They make rude comments when I put her coat and boots on in inclement weather!"

"Of course, how terrible, please continue," I said, mustering up as much empathy as I could without locking into a 'tweek-your-cheek' grin.

"Do you have a photo?" asked Ms. Walker.

"Why of course, here she is!" proudly replied Percy.

'I'll be damned!' I thought as the photo finally made its way to me. 'A *professional* photo with one of those bench-in-the-park backgrounds!'

"My problem," Percy continued, "is if the neighbors succeed and get the building changed into a condo, it will be a 'no pets allowed' condo! What will I DO?" he sobbed.

'Move, maybe?' I thought covertly to myself.

The empathic, pained look on the other group members' faces was impressive. You'd think they just heard that Ebola wiped out New York City or something. The pained look rapidly changed into a 'what-in-the-hell-are-you-talking-about-nitwit' look when I ventured forth the idea:

"*People* are the boss and not *cats*."

Very long silence.

"I mean it's *our* responsibility to guide *them* and make *them* happy!" I confabulated in a nick of time.

Mental lightbulbs began to illuminate as if someone was turning up a dimmer switch. Lights on! Smiles! Nodding heads! I did it!

"That's *absolutely* right!" exclaimed Ms. Guiliani.

"How *insightful*!" bubbled Mrs. Grobman.

"Brilliant, right on!" chimed in Percy Nottingham.

"You bet your doctor-lovin' ass!" declared Ethel in her famously less-than-subtle approach (perhaps indicative of underactive prefrontal lobes).

'Aha, bonding achieved. Therapeutic breakthrough. Now what?' I pondered as some additional cat chat ensued without much further direction.

"Next session we'll pick one of the problems that we mentioned today and then employ a group process to solve it," I stated optimistically.

'Nice touch,' I thought—'hey, being a cat psychologist ain't so bad!'

As the group rose to leave, I noticed they were still showing each other photos, trading Meow-Mix coupons, and providing tons of empathy. I had always thought housecats were schizophrenic or at least nutty as hell, but now I had to rethink that long-held belief.

"Crazy like a fox," old Herbie Freedman used to say.

What other animal could reduce humans to such a subservient state, without the humans having a clue as to what was happening? Not only that, cats don't have to do *anything*! No 'fetch the paper,' protect the house (never have seen a 'beware of the cat' sign), retrieve a ball or frisbee, assist blind individuals, sniff out bombs or drugs, or ride around in the back of police cars! Nada! Okay, maybe they occasionally will chase a wad of paper or a string, and give a meow or two. They can even turn on the tickle-me-Elmo like purring machine to the delight of their owners, usually a minute before drawing blood with a merciless, unprovoked clawing frenzy. Hell, the only reason they use litter boxes is because they're too lazy to go out (especially in inclement weather) and they like to dig in clay. Most everything they do is to get something *they* want! Even when they rub their haunches on their owners' legs it has a purpose—i.e., pick me up, feed me, rub my neck, I'm too tired to jump up on the sofa, etc.

I sat and mused a bit more.

The session reminded me of the cat Mom kept in the basement— named P.C. (a name that I had cleverly derived from 'pussycat'). We kept it there to catch mice—seems like everyone in Fairview had mice (or rats). P.C. used to proudly bring them in her mouth to the foot of the cellar stairs. This usually prompted my mother to *ascend* the stairs quite rapidly—like in about .2 seconds to be exact. P.C. did better than old Rusty the dog, though. He typically would put the mice in his water dish—they never did swim well, so we typically found them sort of floating. We had an ample supply of mice, so there was enough for both animals. Unfortunately, that was about the only constructive thing that P.C. did. This was in stark contrast to Rusty who actually won Best Trick Dog in the Kid's Kennel Ration dog show (even though he never ate Kennel Ration—he always ate a combination of chopped meat and carrots—dogs needed vegetables too, my mother insisted). Rusty's claim to fame was singing (a.k.a. howling) to the Wrigley's Spearmint chewing gum jingle on TV. In one of the first flashes of brilliance that would become the harbinger of my later professional skills, I somehow coerced him to howl as soon as I began the 'boom, boom, boom, look for the spear and get chewing enjoyment...' jingle (shaping or successive approximations in psychology talk). Didn't even know it was psychology at the time. I also had Henry the Easter duck imprint on me and follow me around the neighborhood just like Conrad Lorenz—much to the amazement of many of the broom-wielding neighbors (but that's another story!)

P.C. also howled. She would emit these blood-curdling, terrifying howls at certain times. Sounded like she was possessed or something, making me consider a call to the Ladies in Black for an exorcism. The howling was usually accompanied by the cat trying to walk in a very unusual manner, raising her rear end even higher in the air every time my father used to yell at it to shut up. Mom used to say the cat was in heat. I had no clue as to what she was talking about, particularly because in the winter it was *freezing* down in that basement!

"Well, Dr. Wayward, how did the group go?" asked Connie.

"Fine, fine, they really seemed to click." I replied, drifting back to reality.

"Say, my cat, Mittens, is pulling her hair out….do you think it's psychological?"

Yet another long silence.

Then I though of Dougie and the cats…..

CHAPTER 6
Dougie and the 'Hood

"Glint, Dougie's here," warbled Mom.

Dougie McGuartney lived up the block, but it was still part of the neighborhood. He was an unusual kid, even by Fairview standards. Most of us called him "Boola," although for the life of me I have no idea how he acquired that name. Dougie hated cats and chased them at every opportunity. Dougie also was into droopy, baggy pants well before it was cool to have droopy, baggy pants. It seemed like they were always on the cusp of falling down, and in those days that was *not* a fashion statement (and Dougie was *not* a plumber). Actually, what it did state was that Dougie typically was wearing his older brother's hand-me-down pants. In fact, on one of the famous Fairview Fourth of July three-legged races, Dougie and Warren (allegedly the fastest kid in town) almost got killed when Dougie's pants slipped precariously low, causing him to walk like a penguin before biting the dust (with Warren in tow). Dougie also wore a ratty Yankees baseball cap. In today's terms, Dougie would be called a slob. Actually, many people called him that back then, but not to his face—Dougie had a wicked headlock!

Dougie was really good at box ball. The rule of box ball was that you had to bounce a Spalding (aka "spaldeen") rubber ball (costing 25 cents) on one bounce at a wall, keeping the rebound within a sidewalk box—a variant of side-by-side tennis. Dougie must have been the originator of the moon, or at least the plumber's crack. I think it may have been a diversionary tactic—the opponents were hysterical with laughter, but ol' Dougie doggedly kept whacking the ball. We were all easily amused in those days. Dougie routinely came over to get me to play, me all the while knowing that not only would I lose at box ball, but I would be mooned at least 15 times during the course of the game. Plus, Dougie put mysterious "English" on the ball causing it to bounce in unpredictable ways, this due to holding his hand in a karate chop manner.

Dougie lived in a rather ramshackle place. Given the fact that we *all* lived in less-than-opulent conditions, calling his place ramshackle meant it was *really* bad. At any given time, the place was surrounded with several dozen cats—big cats, little cats, fat cats, skinny cats. Some even had unusual features like no tail or one eye. In retrospect, many of the cats most likely were closely related—too close. We used to wonder if Chan, the guy that owned Chan's Dragon Palace, would occasionally snatch a couple of the heftier felines to secretly round out his menu. This rumor typically intensified when the cat census mysteriously dipped and the restaurant had nightly specials. We never worried about Dougie's house having mice. Heck, you could smell the cats a mile away! This occurred despite the fact that Mrs. McGuartney was always chasing the cats with a broom, wailing at them with a vengeance. Maybe that's why Dougie did it too (another early breakthrough of psychological insight for young Glint—"modeling"!!). Sometimes we would sit across the street and bet baseball cards on how many cats she would actually hit in any given fracas. Once she hit at least a dozen with one swing—Eddie said they were cornered. It was particularly entertaining when several were in "heat" (that perplexing term again), doing their funny walk and howling while simultaneously ducking from the potentially lethal swoop of the broom. Dougie's Mom used to scream at the cats in Italian. Dougie was another Irish-Italian kid in a geographic locale with many of similar genetic stock.

Many of us prided ourselves in our ability to 'speak' Italian. We typically repeated phrases overheard when some of the older neighbors argued and threw stuff at each other, or chased animals with brooms. We took particular delight in trying out our new verbal acquisitions by yelling one of the spanking-new, novel phrases at an unsuspecting elder.

"Gubbidust!" I yelled, not having a clue as to what I had just screamed.

"You badda boy! I tella you mudda!" was Mr. Rinaldi's reply.

I just *knew* whatever I said had to be good, based on the redness of his face and the rapid, high intensity arm movements. Dougie was much better than any of us in yelling Italian cuss words—he was simply a savant in that regard. He even used to try out stuff with his mother, often prompting her to begin chasing *him* with the broom, granting the cats a temporary reprieve. We also bet baseball cards on how many times she would whack Dougie on the head. A frequent side bet was placed on whether she would knock his Yankees baseball hat off.

"Ah fungool," was his favorite. He said he knew the English translation, which, in actuality, was rather easy to deduce. He said it famously, with crisp, gutteral enunciation.

Dougie also had to spit all the time. He was highly skilled in this endeavor as well, being able to squirt saliva several yards from the gap between his two front teeth. Little white wads of liquid death, traveling at a blazing velocity—faster than light. Then—SPLAT! Dougie's spitting prowess was legendary. For the life of me though, I couldn't figure out how he kept himself so well hydrated—I figured he had to load up on water the night before.

Dougie also cussed in English—all the time in fact. His favorite by far was the legendary '*f-word*.' F-word this, f-word that! Seemed like every sentence had to have at least one f-word. Sometimes there were so many f-words that the sentences didn't make any sense.

"F**k this f***in' f**k shit!" he would say.

No idea what he was talking about, but he was emphatic and apparently agitated.

"F***in' great!"—he'd say when he was happy.

"F***in' shit!"—he'd say when he was mad.

"F***in' whatever!"—he'd say it just to say it.

It sometimes was highly entertaining to watch Dougie talk with his brother, Ralph. Ralph was an f-word meister, beyond reproach. He should have had a big "F" on the front of his tee shirt. It seemed like he and Dougie would often have an f-word-a-thon. It was *amazing* that they would actually *communicate*. I think they must have had innate f-word decoders in their brains. How else would they understand a sentence like:

"F***in' go….f**k….now, up there…F**k. F***in' great man, f***in' funny….later no maybe…f**k….ha, ha, ha."

A veritable cornucopia of F-bombs! No, better yet—a blitzkrieg! And they actually communicated!

Plus, they all spit in between the f-words.

Sometimes they would be joined by Billy Flowers and his cousin, Jess. Then all four of them would launch into an f-word jamboree—here an f-word, there an f-word, everywhere an f-word. No kidding. Occasionally we would be able to decipher a word beginning with a vowel. We often sat and observed, our eyes wide in sheer amazement.

I would not hear of the psychological term, *coprolalia*, until much later.

Hanging around with Dougie and the other guys tended to influence and pressure us into using the same language. Proper usage was a definite sign of coolness! Unfortunately, my father, though able to cuss with the best of them (he was in the Navy at one time), didn't truly appreciate my "f***in' no way" answer to the question of whether I was the one who yelled an Italian cuss word at Mr. Rinaldi.

Lifebuoy soap tasted terrible.

Dougie cut quite a profile strolling down Lincoln Street—drooping pants, untied sneakers (Keds), ratty hat askew, spitting, muttering f-words. Hell, he was ahead of his time in so many ways! Dougie strolling down Lincoln Street reminded me of a gunfighter walking down the main drag in Dodge City at high noon (with some allowance for attire). I envisioned furtive glances from behind drawn curtains, blinds closed, people calling their children and small pets and locking the doors. Errico Morricone could have produced the music score for Dougie's stroll. Dougie generally did not mix well with the neighbors.

Dougie had a particularly strained relationship with the Stanonni family. They lived several houses down the block. The Stanonni's often served as the wellspring of picturesque Italian cuss words, as they allegedly had "hot blood" according to overheard adult conversations (held typically when everyone was having a brewski or two). We surmised that it was the hot blood that made them turn red frequently. Mrs. Stannoni was about two times as big as her husband, even though he wore shoes with *very* high heels. He always wore a hat and carried a cane (with which he adroitly chased Dougie frequently, and with finesse).

He also had a handlebar moustache—quite a dapper fellow in his own right—three-piece suits and all. Mr. Stannoni was also very difficult to understand—we often had to determine the intent of his message by the expression on his face and whether he appeared to be sputtering or not.

Most of the Stannoni clan members were a cross between the round shape of Mrs. Stannoni, and Mr. Stannoni's height, giving them the appearance of Weebils. I used to like to mingle with them because I could actually see over the tops of some of their heads (unless they wore hats). Dougie used to really tick them off by calling them munchkins and singing "we're off to see the wizard" or using other similar descriptive and witty phrases.

"Hey you guinea munchkin coot!" Dougie would scream (he did not harbor much respect for elders).

"You bada' boy sonna-da-bitch —I breaka' you ass!" was the reply.

"Hey shrimpboat!" Dougie would respond (what Dougie lacked in creativity, he made up for with spirit).

"I breaka' and kicka' you wisa' ass—I sticka' disa cane upa' dere!" Mr. S. would sputter. I was always intrigued by his intense focus on what he would do to Dougie's derriere. It sounded rather gruesome. He also said other things that we would attempt to remember so as to try out in future encounters with Mr. Rinaldi.

I was very careful to stay out of cane range, particularly since Dougie was cat-like in his ducking agility—and he had to use these skills to their limit. Sometimes after missing Dougie with a few swings, Mr. Stannoni would swing so hard that he would lose his balance (maybe because of those enormous heels) and go into a gyroscope-like spin, sputtering like crazy. Once he hit the horse chestnut tree head on, squashing the brim of his hat.

We all stood there as if in shock.

I immediately had to go inside to change my pants.

Mr. and Mrs. Stannoni had a son, Lennie. He was about three inches taller than Mr. S., making him a towering 4'10" or so. Lennie was a nice guy and all (even though Philip called him a dimwit), but he often bore the brunt of the mysterious Italian cuss words that echoed throughout that household. A Stannoni Italian cuss-out was particularly entertaining during the summer months in the days before air conditioning. Many such tirades were related to his intelligence, which we determined was somewhat lacking by information gleaned from others (in addition to Philip). Lennie never drove a car (I was convinced he couldn't see over the steering wheel). He did like cats, in fact, he was like the pied piper of the Lincoln Street feline corps. Some people liked pigeons, some people liked goldfish, but Lennie *really* liked cats. He used to bring pans of milk out, making the cats follow him around in a parade for amazingly long periods of time before putting the pans on the ground. Sometimes he would play his transistor radio and have the cats follow, alleging that they were marching to the music. Lennie was also easily amused.

Lennie was older than us (at least chronologically) by quite a few years and he did, however, have a spanking-new motorscooter! A fine piece of machinery that was the envy of the young, Lincoln Street denizens! Lennie would sit on it in his driveway and sometimes even kick start the vehicle and repeatedly rev it up—in a roaring (sort of) putt, putt, putt (the sound resembling a weed whacker that hadn't been invented yet). Or he would polish it until it gleamed. One day I was sitting on the front porch waiting for Dougie, when I, by chance, gazed up to the top of the hill. Garfield Street ran downhill and intersected Lincoln Street in a "T" at the curb right in front of the house. That day, at the top of the hill, in majestic glory, was LENNIE! On his motorscooter! On the sidewalk! Revving like a madman! With a helmet, goggles, gloves, and a SCARF! With the wind snappily blowing his scarf, Lennie cut quite a noble figure in the brilliant sunlight! A thoroughly striking vision! I heard the putt-putt-putt staccato of the motorscooter that increased to a whining roar and Lennie was off—coming down the sidewalk at breakneck speed, scarf flapping in the wind, helmet gleaming in the sunlight. A glorious testimony to motorscootering if there ever was one!

"F***in' look at that!" blurted Dougie in stark amazement.

Lennie revved up the motorbike even more, shifted (I think) and then Lennie suddenly disappeared— into Mrs. Clerico's hedges! Gone, just like that—in the blink of an eye! Stunning silence! The only clue of Lennie's whereabouts was the gaping space in the hedges and the faint exhaust trailers wafting upward. I strained to hear a reassuring putt-putt,— but nothing! A few moments later I heard twigs snapping and Lennie slowly emerged from the shrubbery. He had leaves and twigs all over himself, his goggles were crooked, and his scarf was missing. There was no scooter, but he still had his gloves on. Lennie produced a tirade of the Italian cuss-words, some of which had never been heard before. The volume and complexity was only rivaled by Mrs. Clerico's less-than-empathic response:

"What the hell are you doing to my hedges you moron?!?! Get that piece of shit outta' here—you're payin' for this!!!"

The majestic bike—now reduced to a piece of shit! With that I had to go inside and change my pants again.

"Evil Stannoni" (that was Dougie's clever name in reference to Evil Kneivel) and his death-defying ride became neighborhood lore. I never did see Lennie ride the scooter again, although soon after the journey into the shrubbery I did hear a conversation, melodically drifting from the Stannoni domicile:

"That mota' bika' is a pizza' shit!"

"You poppa isa right! You gonna' killa youself on that pizza' shit!"

"Yeah and you breaka' you ass too! And if you breaka' you ass I breaka' you ass after that—Sonnafa' bitch!"

That mota' bike was never seen again.

Across the street from the Stannoni's lived Mrs. Burton. She was a white-haired, *BIG*, German woman. It seemed like everyone in the town was defined by nationality and its assumed trappings:

---Greeks (they had a big church on Henry Street and a stranglehold on the deli business [except for Charlie's]).

---Yugoslavians—(aka Yugos) —reputation for having the most family members living in any given house at any one time, and also buying real estate like crazy.

---Polish—(aka Polacks) significant questions were raised about the intellectual prowess, played in oompah bands. They produced delicious sausages.

---Italians—(aka Guineas or whops), usually were criticized covertly, because 80% of the town was at least partly of Italian lineage and most could understand at least some Italian cuss words.

---Irish—(aka Micks) Irish extraction lent itself to a multitude of jokes about potatoes, and beer or vice versa. Mention of this ethnicity also frequently raised intellectual prowess questions.

---Jews—(aka Kikes) prompted statements regarding frugal spending patterns and probiscus size.

---Germans (aka Krauts)—frequently played accordions, drank big glasses of beer, and had neat front lawns with ceramic woodland animals and gnomes.

---Blacks (aka—the less-than-original n-word), not much said because only one black person lived in town, and he was rumored to be 90 years old, lived in a converted barn without plumbing, and purportedly was a descendent of slaves.

Back to Mrs. Burton. She also used to chase Dougie with a broom, joining in the gala neighborhood past-time. Actually, despite looking like Brunhilde, she was pretty damn agile and could wield that broom like a pro. No simple, whop-him-over-the-head techniques for Mrs. B.—she used *both* ends, flailing at Dougie like a windmill (or a ninja)! Dougie said he was sure she had been a Nazi guard woman or something like that. We believed Dougie. Mrs. Burton hated cats—Dougie said she had hundreds of them buried in her yard (I always thought the area was simply her vegetable garden). Everyone used to say that she put arsenic in the vacant lot next to her house to kill the cats. We used to hold our breath whenever we ran through the lot. Actually, we didn't know exactly what arsenic was, but we were *sure* it must be bad. It was a pretty big lot too, and we often would get dizzy by the time we crossed it due to lack of oxygen. Eddie lasted longer because he put a tissue over his mouth and nose. Dougie said he saw arsenic once, but his description resembled mothballs.

Mrs. Burton also had a cookoo clock (again allegedly from Switzerland—that place close to Hoboken) and she had *canaries*. She said that they sang, but I never heard them. They just jumped around the cage and produced enormous amounts of droppings. She used to cover them with a towel when visitors came over, alleging strangers frightened the birds into *not* singing. Both cookoo clocks and canaries were ubiquitous on Lincoln Street. I bet if Charlie Grieger opened a store and just sold cookoo clocks, canaries, brooms, and beer, he would have made a killing! Mrs. Burton used to send me to the store a great deal. Unfortunately, I used to earn five or ten cents per trip (I liked going to the store for Mrs. Fay much better, she was a twenty five to fifty-center).

When I complained about Mrs. B's stinginess to my mother, she would always tell me that Mrs. Burton thought it was a lot of money, that she was old, that I was doing a good deed, she was affected by the Great Depression (another term that we knew absolutely nothing about), yada yada—none of which was even remotely convincing. Because Mrs. Burton was such a formidable figure (big *German* woman, former Nazi, broommeister), I was damned if I were going to ask her for more money! Dougie did once. He said her face turned red, she muttered something (not Italian), and she went for the broom. Dougie reportedly left quickly, prior to witnessing her full response.

Seems like everyone on Lincoln Street wielded brooms for one reason or another. By rights, it should have been the cleanest place in town—or the most dangerous if you were Dougie or a cat. The neighborhood could have fielded a platoon of women with brooms to march in the Fourth of July parade, stepping in unison right behind the school safety patrol band as it belted out 'Moon Over Miami' (for the 63rd time that day). More on that later.

Next door to Mrs. Burton allegedly lived two sisters—the Cardinales. 'Allegedly' because none of us actually *saw* them—at least not both of them at the same time! Dougie said they had an underground tunnel straight to Charlie's deli, and that's how they got food. Again, Dougie was convincing—and the rest of us were gullible, accepting that line of reasoning fairly readily. I once tried to scope out the area behind Charlie's counter for a trap door, but was unsuccessful. Somebody *had* to live there, though, because the newspaper disappeared sometime during the morning. Dougie, in an attempt to lay the matter to rest, periodically would ring the doorbell and run away, hiding across the street to see if anyone popped out. Once he thought he saw someone, but that sighting was never verified. At least no one chased Dougie with a broom on that occasion.

Then there was Paulie Gordman. Paulie lived around the corner, next to Charlie's deli. He was a *very* big kid—he must have been over six feet tall in the 4th grade. He took a size 13 shoe, and for some reason, he always had a flattop haircut that accentuated his already prominent ears. In retrospect there was something genetically askew with Paulie. Stated simply, Paulie was not very smart—and that IS saying it simply (and nicely). Despite his size, I used to beat Paulie up on a fairly regular basis in frenzied rounds of fisticuffs and other street-wise techniques. He was a sucker for a good, jaw-crunching headlock. A well-placed jaw cruncher would reduce Paulie to a blubbering fool—albeit a *large* blubbering fool. You had to jump really high to get him in the headlock. Sometimes I missed and wound up choking his leg, or worse yet, landing on the ground and knocking the wind out of myself. In such instances, I would yell "truce." That would usually confuse Paulie long enough for me to re-ventilate. I don't think Paulie knew what truce actually meant—he probably thought it was Italian for "God said you have to stop or you die" or something else really important.

Paulie always had bad stuff happen to him. He was like that guy in the Al Capp/Little Abner comics who had the black cloud hanging over him all the time—Joe P with a lot of consonants following the 'P'. In regard to Paulie, *he* would get caught shoplifting (once he stole a D battery); *he* crashed into the side of a moving car while running across the street (the car sustained minor damage); *he* got caught when we dropped water balloons on cars from the overpass (we ran faster than he did); *he* would wind up turning his sled left into traffic when we would zoom down the hill by the billboards (everyone else would turn right—in retrospect, I'm not sure if Paulie ever had the left-right thing down); *he* was the one who got hit in the head with a rock when we climbed the cliffs (actually, it bounced off his head and hit Eddie Pressioto, causing Eddie to require

10 stitches); *he* cut his finger with the pocketknife that he brazenly smuggled into school (necessitating a trip to the nurse from hell, Mrs. Teevan); *he* fell in the lake when we went fishing (he screamed that he couldn't swim and had to be pulled out, even though the water was two feet deep at max). These attributes (in addition to being a sucker for the aforementioned headlock) made Paulie an excellent accomplice when we engaged in moderately delinquent behaviors—biggest, slowest, most obvious, dullest, and most suggestible. The suggestible part was particularly attractive, as we often talked Paulie into selling us his brother's stuff—at bargain prices to boot! I once picked up an excellent football helmet for $1.50, much to the chagrin of his brother, Artie. Dougie said that one time he was selling triple-packs of baseball cards for 25 cents per triple pack or three triple packs for a dollar—Paulie bought at the three for a dollar sale price (although Paulie later vehemently denied it). Paulie also was not good at math.

We used to like to play cards with Paulie, some Italian game called "breeshke" (no one could spell it). I can't remember Paulie *ever* winning. If he'd get close to doing so (most likely by pure luck as he had even more problems with the rules than with the left-right thing), we'd simply change the rules a bit. He also frequently lost his (and his brother's) baseball cards when we'd flip for them (made all the more tragic by the inflated price he allegedly would pay to Dougie for the cards originally). Too bad he was too tall to reach down in order to play boxball. Paulie was a paperboy once, but for some reason it never occurred to him that he had to turn in the money he collected from his customers to pay for the papers. For unbeknownst reasons, Paulie quit hanging around with us from junior high school onward. Dougie said Paulie went to jail. He was again convincing.

Many years later, I was back in the neighborhood visiting the family. I recall sitting on the porch stairs gazing at the spot where Lennie abruptly, but magnificently ended his mota' bike career, when I noticed this huge figure loping down the hill, waving frantically and yelling something unintelligible.

"Gllllennnntttt…meeee…..ie…."

I peered intensely, fearing the worst.

"Glllllnnntttt….mmeee….garble, garble, pllleeee."

Damn it was Lurch on his way to tear me limb from limb! All the time looming larger and larger!

"Glint…it's me, your friend, Paulie!" the huge figure finally said in an intelligible manner.

It was incredible— Paulie *grew even more*! "Well I'll be damned! How're you doing big guy?" I said.

"Fine. I'm workin' for the Public Works department (the guys with no teeth and guinea rolls). I was a boxer for a while, but I retired."

'Boxer?' I thought to myself. It would have been a major feat for Paulie to master the ol' one-two—not to mention several one-two's in rapid succession. His corner man would have gone nuts trying to get Paulie to use his right or left punch on cue (due to that right/left problem). On the up side, Paulie did have a hard head (Eddie Pressioto would attest to that!).

"Good for you!" I said jovially, while thinking I must have been out of my mind to pick fights with this guy when I was a kid—sort of like David versus Godzilla.

"Would like to talk more. Have to go— I 'm the bartender at Patsy's!"

"Take care big guy!"

'Hope no one needs change for a twenty,' I thought.

CHAPTER 7

Yet Another Session—A Visit with Eugene

"Well, Eugene, how have things gone this week?"

"Mumble."

"What's that?"

"Mumble, murrfff, mumble."

"Sorry, I can't understand what you're saying"

"Just friggin' fine, Doc!"

'Ah, Eugene,' I thought, 'such a crisp, cogent, communicator!'

"How has school been going?" I asked.

"Didn't go this week," he replied.

"Why didn't you go?"

"Why should I?" he puffed.

"Why shouldn't you?" I retorted.

"Why do you ask?"

"Why do you ask why I ask?"

"Why do you want to know why I ask why you ask?"

"Who's on first?" I slipped in.

"What the hell you talkin' about?......"

'Going to be a ring-around-the-rosy session,' I thought.

Another session from hell with old Eugene. Eugene Hill is a 16 year-old, lanky, acneed, earringed adolescent. I never could tell his actual hair color—this week it was green on top, ringed with black below. A big clump of green curls sat atop bands of closely-shaved black hair. Reminded me of a raccoon that had a bad joke played on it while it was sleeping. Eugene also sported earrings; ten on each ear to be exact (I counted them once when he was in one of his no-speak phases). He also had a ring in his nose and some kind of tie-bar like apparatus going through the bridge of his nose (reminded me of old National Geographics that I used to check out of the elementary school library so as to view native women from the Belgian Congo with bare breasts). Eugene indicated that he had other parts of his body pierced and I simply took his word for it.

Eugene also sported tattoos. One was in the form of a chain around his neck. Another on his skinny arm was a devil's face—except the girth of his arm made it look like a pinhead. He said he had others, but I took his word for that too. I guess his parents gave the okay for that. He wore a leather string necklace with an ankh attached, fingernail polish on two fingers of each hand, several rings, tattered, very large pants and *huge*, untied Nikes or Adidas (too dirty to tell) that each must have weighed 14 lbs. and had three inch soles. I was surprised that he could walk with those things—they each were the size of a shoebox! A Frankenstein-ish look if there ever was one! The ensemble was topped off with a tie-dyed t-shirt (I recalled that such a fine shirt would look much better at Woodstock with bell bottoms and platform shoes).

"Hey, hey we're the Monkees," I hummed to myself.

"Okay Doc, so maybe things didn't go so good," Eugene finally 'fessed up.

"What do you mean?" I asked as I came back to reality.

"Well, I sorta' got kicked out so I didn't go."

"You sorta' got *kicked out* and *then* you didn't go?"

"Yeah, somethin' like that," Eugene replied rather meekly.

"If you got kicked out, you couldn't go if you *wanted* to!" I said in a seemingly logical fashion.

"Just not to class," Eugene replied.

"Where else could you go?" I asked incredulously.

"Parking lot."

"Oh, that sounds good, get a little street education—mota bike 101!" I said, perhaps a tad sarcastically.

"What the hell is a friggin' *mota bike*?"

"Make that automotive engineering 101," I replied.

"Ho, ho, ho, Doc—real funny, man! A real knee-slapper!" he replied in his best Eddie Murphy impersonation. "*They* won't let me in!"

"Why?" I asked somewhat confused.

"Because they're friggin' a-holes! That's why!" was the response.

"Anything you might have done to bring out their *a-holedness* ?" I asked.

Silence.

"Let me rephrase that—what *did* you do?"

Look of consternation.

"Hello, Eugene?"

"Okay, so maybe I did a little something—but they overreacted!" he whined.

"Just what *did* you do?" I asked.

"Called in a bomb threat," he said tersely.

"You called in a *bomb threat?*" I croaked, in my attempt to act as neutral and non-incredulous as possible.

"Yeah, but I was only pranking."

'I'm sure they saw the humor in that,' I mused.

"Where did you call it in from?"

"The phone booth across the street from school."

"Green hair give you away?" I blurted out without even thinking.

"Maybe. But I didn't use my cellphone."

"Who did you call?" I asked, trying to regain my neutrality.

"Principal," was Eugene's reply.

"Doesn't his office overlook the area in front of the school building?"

"Uh, yeah, probably."

"So do you think he might have become just a tad suspicious when he looked out and saw a kid with green hair who should be in school, laughing his rear end off in a phone booth across the street at the exact time a phone call about a bomb was coming in?" I asked. "Very clever there buddy. Should go down in the Prank Hall of Fame… So how about we invite your parents in now and get their take on this?"

Eugene was by no means a happy camper at this juncture.

Connie escorted Mr. and Mrs. Hill in. Mr. Jerome Hill was a short, portly, balding man in his late 40's who sported a polyester-looking three-piece suit. Mrs. Iris H. was a buxom, overly made up woman with a dress cut to display her assets, pumps, and some kind of platinum, beehive hairdo. She was an icon of the '70's! Mrs. H. had a penchant for leaning over so as to afford me a gander at the dangling, bulbous assets at least six times per session (which I had to do discreetly so as not to let Eugene or his dad think I was distracted or anything).

So, folks, what do *you* think about Eugene's suspension?" I asked, subtly looking askance at the assets.

"Friggin' assholes!" replied Mrs. Hill in a minimally lady-like manner (causing the assets to jiggle wildly). "Eugene wouldn't have done nothing like that!"

"Didn't he *admit* to doing so?" I asked, admiring the striking family resemblance in dialogue style.

"They *made* him say he did it! Now his grades are shot to hell!"

"But weren't his grades already shot before this happened?" I inquired.

"Yes," squeaked up Mr. H. It was quite obvious the he was *not* the big kahuna of the Hill family. Probably had something to do with assets, I'm sure.

"So you agree that Eugene was in dire straits before the not-so-anonymous phone call?"

"Absolutely! He simply didn't give a damn about his studies!" replied Jerome.

"It's all bullshit!" Eugene chimed in.

"He's right!" echoed Mrs. Hill.

"Right about what?" I asked. 'Hmmm, a coalition here,' I thought, commending myself for the keen insight, 'Mom and Eugene versus Dad. Not too much doubt as to who would win out—assets or not.'

"What have you tried to do to "encourage" Eugene to produce academically?" I asked.

"*Everything!*" moaned Mrs. H.

"Could you be a bit more specific?" I pleaded.

"We took the telephone away," stated Iris proudly.

"And?"

"He used *our* cell phones," Mr. H said laconically. "I was getting texts from his friends! Even sexting! But then we grounded him."

"And?" I asked hopefully.

"He snuck out the window," replied Mr. H. in a hope-dashing manner.

"Then what did you do?"

"We took the car away," replied Mrs. H., again leaning over precariously (her ability to sit back up again while fighting gravity was incredible!)

"Now you're talking!" I replied emphatically, even though a flunking 16-year-old owning a vehicle is a bit much.

"How did that work?"

"He took our car keys and wouldn't give them to us until we gave him *his* keys back. We had to go to work, so we traded," Mr. Hill replied rather meekly.

"Safe to say it didn't work?" I asked.

"It sucked!" volunteered Eugene.

"Yes, that's probably another way of describing it," I muttered. "So what might be a motivator for Eugene?"

"Money! M-o-n-e-y." glowered Eugene.

"Yes, that's what we do now," Mr. H. responded, "Five dollars a day to go to school, two dollars if he stays there the entire day, two dollars if there's no detention, three dollars if he does his work in school, and five dollars more if he completes his homework."

'Seventeen dollars a day for acting like 99% of the other 16-year-olds in town (who do it for free). Not bad Eugene. Not hard to see who's leading this parade!' I thought to myself.

"Sounds like quite a bit of change for a day's work—where did you come up with this idea?" I asked.

"Eugene's previous counselor, Mr. Swartz," said Mr. H. in a muffled voice.

I had forgotten that the family had seen a counselor before, for about two or three years. Rasputin Swartz—a licensed clinical professional counselor of some type. I think he got one of those mail-order degrees from El Nino of the Pacific University in California. I heard about him before, and not in glowing terms. Several disgruntled patients, seeking second opinions relayed tales that were strikingly similar. One of the classics was that he told a mother (actually several mothers) that if the kid bit her, she should bite him back. This caused a great deal of embarrassment when bite marks were discovered by one child's preschool teacher, where the child alluded to the fact that his mother was in a satanic cult and tried to eat him. This also produced havoc in the local grocery store, when, after biting her child back a mother was soundly whacked four times in the back of the head with a box of Fiber One by an 80-year old good Samaritan. Another bit of wisdom disseminated by Rasputin was that if the child acts up in a store, the parents should act up even more so as to embarrass the child and make him stop. This ploy unfortunately resulted in one set of parents being pepper-sprayed and handcuffed by police officers and escorted out of the local K-Mart. Reportedly, they decided to throw their own temper tantrums right in front of the flashing blue light, thereby coming to the attention of a horde of shoppers and the store manager who was doing the announcing. The end result was not pretty.

Rasputin Swartz had children of his own; two I think. The 10-year-old got in trouble for burning down the neighbor's tool shed—with the neighbor's cat inside it. He also periodically torched various pieces of ornamental shrubbery, thereby giving the Swartz yard that Mt. St. Helen's look. The younger one put a clock radio in the microwave, the resulting arrival of fire trucks and smoke damage causing the family to be evicted from their rented townhouse. The mention of Jerome or Jordon Swartz's name struck fear in the hearts of teachers, babysitters, and neighbors (especially those with small pets or ornamental shrubbery). Rasputin's favorite quote—"Kids will be kids—I was like that once"—tells all. Getting back to the new Hill incentive program—

"Hmmm….So does the payment schedule work?" I asked.

"If he needs money, it works like a charm," Mr. H. stated proudly.

"He does like the bonuses!" crooned Mrs. H.

"Bonuses?" I repeated in an 'oh, no, what's next?' manner.

"Yes, Eugene requested an additional five dollar bonus if he did *all* the things he was supposed to do," Mrs. H stated, in conjunction with the nodding of Mr. H.

'Now he's up to $22!' I mused. 'That's 110 dollars a week! No allowance-slouch this guy!—An allowance bonanza!'

"So, Eugene, if you're getting this much money, why don't you simply take care of business?"

"Bored" he replied in a bored fashion.

"Bored?" I replied incredulously.

"Yeah, like if I get a lot of money, I can sock some of it away and sorta' take a vacation from the contract for a week or two," stated Eugene in a monotonic manner.

"When the money runs out, I play the game and do the good stuff again for a while."

"Can I ask what you do with all that money anyway?" I ventured.

"No." Eugene replied curtly.

"He spends it like Mr. Bigshot," interjected Mr. Hill.

"But he *needs* things," whined Mrs. H emphatically.

"Seventy-five dollar jeans that look like rats chewed them? And baggy at that—like he got them from the circus after the clown died! Or is it the cellular phone—or the iPod—or the $115 dollar athletic shoes that look like he stole them from the Transformers? Gas money?" asked Mr. Hill, probably not expecting an answer.

"No, *we* buy him all that stuff, remember?" Mrs. Hill said in an unusually meek fashion. "He uses his money for *other* things."

'Drugs, sex and rock and roll,' I thought, 'Definitely in charge of the parade.'

"So it's fair to say that the program may have some glitches," I stated in a therapeutically summarizing fashion.

"You might say that—just a bit, though," replied Mrs. H.

"I can live with it," piped up Eugene.

"Ever think of using The Club to lock his steering wheel?" I asked.

Eugene almost went through the ceiling with that one. Major staredown (i.e., I will wish bad things happen to you and your firstborn) techniques were being employed.

"Er, we can't exactly," peeped Mr. Hill.

"Why?"

"Eugene took away our set of keys for his car—he locks it and we can't get in there to put the club on the steering wheel."

"It's my damn car—you'd don't need keys to *my* car!" bellowed Eugene.

"Not just *any* car either, it's a damn Jeep Grand Cherokee—almost new at that!" growled Mr. Hill who seemed to be getting a bit redder as the session progressed.

"But it doesn't have navigation!" Eugene said ruefully.

"I told you we'd get you that for your birthday," insisted Mrs. Hill.

"But that's six months away!" protested Eugene.

"Well, if you're good maybe we'll get it earlier," Mrs. H. responded.

"Yeah, okay, sure, bueno, righto" he replied.

'Multilingual,' I thought.

"And maybe if you stick to your curfew too," ventured Mr. H.

"What time is curfew?" I asked, bracing for the worst.

"Between one and two a.m.," replied Mrs. H., "but sometimes we have to text him as a reminder."

"I want to make it more like midnight after that fiasco two weeks ago," said Mr. Hill. He went to a party with his school buddies. Turned out to be a keg party, with the keg supplied by one of his friend's parents. Eugene got a bit carried away and we discovered him on the front lawn. His sweater was on backwards, vomit on his clothes, no shoes, just lying there with this stupid look on his face. I had to take his pulse because he wasn't moving. He was situated in between the ceramic deer and mushrooms, his head in between the deer's hind legs, looking up. (I don't recall if the Hills were German, with the lawn decorations and all). When I finally roused him, he insisted he had gotten sick from sushi. Only reason we know he was out there was because we heard squealing tires, blasting rap music, and kids yelling."

"What were the consequences?" I asked hopefully, once again.

"He was grounded for Saturday and Sunday—but he was probably too sick to go anywhere on Saturday anyway."

"But he said he was *sorry!*" said Mrs. H. defensively, "And he did clean up around the mushrooms!"

"Edna, it *rained*—that's how the yard got cleaned!" retorted Mr. H.

"Folks you two seem to differ on what you feel are appropriate consequences," I said, all the while thinking, 'sheesh.'

"Damn straight we do! He should go to military school or foster care or something!" exploded Mr. Hill in an uncharacteristically dramatic fashion.

Surprisingly, Eugene sat passively.

"Eugene is a good kid (my fingers were crossed), he's just making bad choices," I ventured in my best psychological try-to-garner-support manner. "I suggest we come up with a written contract for the school problem."

"Eugene told me he'd try—we don't need to write it out!" insisted Mrs. Hill, assets bouncing delightfully wildly once again.

"I still think….."

"Nahh, Doc, I'll try real hard," drawled Eugene. "Have to go now."

'Do his work and get a Porsche next,' I thought.

Eugene was all smiles. Mrs. Hill was all smiles. Mr. Hill was even smiling. Hell I even was smiling, but that was because the session was over. Eugene wins, the parents are clueless, but at least everyone's happy. Great therapeutic strides. Diagnosis: chronic cluelessness coupled with adolescent adjustment issues (with a dash of budding sociopathy).

The family rose and shuffled toward the door. I noticed the seat of his jeans indeed looked like a rat or some other furry, gnawing creature had chewed them—offset nicely by boxer shorts of which 75% showed. I overheard Eugene mentioning that he needed a new subwoofer for his car and a 60-inch TV for his room, and Mr. Hill saying that he would look into it. I also heard mention of Wally's Tattoo Heaven.

"See ya' next week Doc," Eugene said as he went out the door.

"No bomb threats, buddy," I replied.

I sat and wondered. Mr. and Mrs. Hill are basically nice people—how had they gone awry? What if Eugene had siblings? What was Eugene's true hair color? What if the Hills had extra car keys made? What if they had thoroughly throttled Eugene a decade ago? What if….

"Dr. Wayward, Mr. Carbone is here," interrupted Connie.

"One minute please," I replied. As I began to reminisce about clothing.

CHAPTER 8
Fairview Fashion Statement

I recall that in about the 5th grade or so, fashion became a major priority, second only to increasing speculation regarding the origins of subtle bumps appearing on some of the female classmates' chests (to be discussed later). Except, of course, for Dougie, who was definitely more interested in the latter, utterly disinterested in the former, and who also made persuasive arguments as to the etiology of the bumps (founded on data gleaned from the occasion in which he had touched Joanie's prior to getting whacked with her math book). I covertly had also seen much larger bumps in Lou Ferrara's magazines. Nonetheless, it was a male thing to try to outdo each other by acquiring the spiffiest clothing, and flaunting the most cutting edge wardrobe. There generally were three ways to acquire such sartorial splendor: (1) Go to the store and buy it; (2) Order the latest fashions from the Sears Roebuck catalogue, or (3) Inherit it from siblings or from older neighbors. Unfortunately in my case, I often fell into last category and the supplier of the haberdashery was none other than BILLY TOWERS!

I was less than fond of receiving clothes from Billy. Typically my mother would come home with several Food Fair grocery bags brimming with clothes and joyfully announce that my back to school wardrobe had arrived (Philip was generally immune from this debacle, as Billy was an ectomorph like me, while Philip was more of the mesomorph genre). Occasionally, some of the stuff would be pretty cool, but mostly it was of the marginal Goodwill variety. Looking back, I think Philip derived perverse satisfaction from my haberdashery tribulations.

"Hey Philip, what do you think of this jacket?" I'd ask.

"Hey that's keen, you're a cool cat—dig it!" he'd reply.

"Really?"

"You bet!" he'd say in a very convincing manner—although he often had to leave the room and weird howling sounds, undoubtedly reflecting poorly stifled, unbridled laughter, emanated from the hallway. He was convincing though, on par with Dougie. The responses to my new duds were a bit different at school, however.

"Hey Glint—nice burgundy wide whale corduroy jacket!" yelled Murph, in between hysterical gasps. Damn, he was almost crying with laughter.

"Goes real good with that pinstripe red shirt and the hush puppies!" (acquired from Little Al's shoe store, I might add) chimed in Louie.

'Damn that Philip!'

"Hey gang—check out Glint's new jacket!"

All this by 8:15 a.m.—I knew the day was rapidly going downhill.

This type of scenario would often be made worse when I would accidentally run into Billy at school, typically when I was accompanied by some of my friends and he, by his upperclassmen cronies. Billy would take particular pains to point out that I was wearing *his* hand-me-downs.

"Glint—wearing my old jacket, eh?" queried Billy as if he didn't know the answer. "I hated that piece of dog dump!"

'What to do?? Say *yes*, and bear the brunt of the condescending look of my peers, their hackles, and their biting, caustic, 5th grade wit—or, say *no* and have Billy rapidly develop a persuasive case with mounting evidence that I was indeed the recipient of the burgundy corduroy jacket and then taunt me with a "swear on the bible" that it wasn't the case. Such is the origin of neuroses!

One particularly incisive, but not novel, comment was made by Murph—a low blow by any standards, and of a nadir-low, utterly devastating magnitude by 5th grade Fairview mores:

"Looks like you got that from the circus after the clown died!"

"Ho, ho, ho!"

'Groan.'

After enduring numerous vignettes like that, with a plethora of low blows, my parents took pity on me and bought new stuff. In retrospect I think that the change in heart was heavily influenced by the fact that Billy Towers hit his adolescent growth spurt and the arms and legs of his garments were fully 6 inches too long, and the waist and chest sizes were overly roomy, causing me to: (1) lose my pants at inopportune times, sometimes tripping in the process; or (2) allowing me to slap Philip with a wet-towel-like smack due to the velocity of the extra half-foot of material in the arms—and I could truthfully say that I technically didn't *touch* him (I did entertain the thought of becoming an attorney at one point). Besides that, Mom's pedal-powered sewing machine never worked so the possibility of alterations was moot.

One of my prized sartorial acquisitions was my spiffy Thom McCann *Snap-jacks!* These shoes came in black, and resembled Dutch Brigadoon fare, but with a snap mechanism in the front. They would have gone well at Plymouth Rock, but snaps weren't invented yet. Sliding on into Mrs. Alexander's math class with my Snap-jacks, outfitted with cleats on the heels (allegedly to reduce wear—actually to make neat clicking sounds wherever you walked) was the epitome of coolness. Of course you really couldn't run with Snap-jacks because after a while the snap mechanism would get loose and open as you picked up speed. Warren, the really fast kid, once used this to his advantage as, upon launching into mind boggling acceleration, the Snap-jack flew off his foot and whacked the pursuing Paulie right square in the forehead.

"Wooo, wooo, clop, clop.

WHACK!!!… ooohhhh." mumbled Paulie…(for some reason Warren would always go "woo-wooo" when running—we never did figure out why!)

Unfortunately, despite his crying, Paulie had the wherewithal to quickly recover Warren's shoe and toss it on the roof of the gymnasium. Warren had a difficult time getting about for the rest of the day, telling the teacher that he lost his shoe at recess and it was nowhere to be found. He subsequently opted for Keds.

The Snap-jacks could be accented by classy Casino pants and white socks. These leggings essentially were regular chinos with some newer designs (like checks) and a small, inverted "v" cut into the center of the seam at the bottom. We assumed they were worn routinely in Las Vegas or something because they had casinos—of course no one really knew where Las Vegas was. Some said it was close to Hoboken. Geographic acumen was generally sparse in Fairview. It was pro forma that these garments were "pegged." Pegged meant tightened to the point that if we were older, we would have spoken several octaves above what we were even speaking now, and our eyes would have resembled those of Walleye Pikes. Pegged also meant that you should not bend over, eat much, or make any sudden movements. Fat kids had a particularly difficult time with pegged pants, tending to resemble bloated sausages, particularly if the pants were of the sharkskin variety. Conversely, skinny kids tended to look like stick men. Casino pants had another drawback—because they sported the inverted "v" on the bottom, they could not be altered. Therefore, more and more white sock began to show after they had been washed a few times—Snap-Jacks, pegged high waders, and white tube socks with the multicolored lines on top—yet another trend setting innovation! Once leg began to show over the socks, it became time to pass the treasured Casinos on down to a younger neighbor on the block— luckily Billy was too tall by then.

Once Jimmie Kolowski decided to make his own Casinos while sitting in Ms. Gundling's English class. He smuggled in a pair of scissors from art class and began to snip away fiendishly at a pair of non-optimal standard fare pants as she droned on with a poem that went:

"I know a place where the sun is like gold…."

'Snip, snip, rip, rip."

"..and the cherry blossoms burst with snow…"

'Snip, snip, snip.'

Unfortunately, because of the clandestine nature of his tailoring efforts done while reciting poetry, Jimmie couldn't get each triangle to match, so he kept widening them and extending the point until it went almost halfway up his leg –sort of like another fashion marvel of the time—clam diggers (made complete with a rope belt, by the way). All of us were complimentary about the dashing self-tailoring, mainly because Jimmie would have whacked us if we weren't. Jimmie never wore the Nuevo-Casinos again, and I suspect his mother whacked him when he got home.

I recall one Easter when I got a gray sharkskin suit from Rogers Brothers in West New York—a literal pantheon of sartorial splendor. Wearing new Easter suits was really big back then. It was pegged to the max—I, a stickman, looked trimmer than ever—heck I even had to hold my breath in order to button them—probably a size 18 waist! This regal wardrobe was rounded out nicely by a pair of black suede shoes purchased at Little Al's Shoe Corner (cleverly named because it *was* on a corner, Al was short, and he *did* sell shoes—that Al sure had a knack for creativity!), white shirt and a skinny black tie. Since it was Easter, and I was an altar boy, I wore the treasured suit under my cassock. At the third genuflection to Deus Omnibus Foreverus, there was a silence-shattering, rip-roaring RRRRIIIIIIPPPPPPP!

Many of the heretofore soporific Ladies in Black, who typically staked out the first several rows, were startled and immediately launched into making signs of the Cross and kicked into overdrive going through their rosaries at warp speed and with mind boggling acumen. It was like turbo-rosaries! I immediately felt my range of movement expand to new horizons, this accompanied by a highly noticeable draft. I had to go home with my jacket tied around my waist, as Father Winci wouldn't let me wear the cassock out of the church. All the way home, Philip kept lifting up my jacket and pointing to the white jockey shorts that now contrasted with the spiffy, gray, sharkskin material. Times like this caused me to truly dislike Philip.

Pegged also extended to the Sears-Roebuck catalogue. It was the kiss of death to have "husky" pants delivered—on par with handouts from Billy Towers! The double-dog disaster would be hand-me-down huskies! One had to be specific and order "slims", lest one resemble Dougie. Some of my fondest childhood memories were sitting on the porch, waiting anxiously for the UPS guy in the brown truck to zip up and deliver a spanking new pair of Sears-Roebuck, green, slim, denims—this experience second only to repeatedly thumbing through the latest catalogue for new selections. Dreams were made of this! I was, however, always perplexed as to why there never were Casino pants advertised.

My second experience with pegged pants gone awry was at the Fairview 4th of July races. My mother got a pair of black pants from the Towers family that actually sort of fit. They were handsomely pegged but were odd in that there were no back pockets. This was a highly suspicious discovery, but Mom convincingly denied that they came from Billy's sister, Pattie—besides she was younger than me and certainly (well, almost) not as tall. Philip kept asking where I was going to put my wallet. I didn't even have a wallet, but this again led me toward a distinct feeling of disaffection regarding my sibling.

That sunny Saturday morning I decided to wear these pants to the annual 4th of July races, held at the Little League field. My first race was the 25-yard dash, and I lined up against Warren, Dougie, Frank, and several other kids. Yes—even DOUGIE! It just so happened that I was a pretty fast skinny kid, and I certainly could give Warren a run for his money (and I didn't wooo-wooo either). The gun fired and everyone took off. I blasted from the starting position, only to be immediately passed up by everyone, including Dougie! My legs wouldn't move! Actually they would move, but only a few inches, restrained by the *pegged pants*! I tried with all my might to move ahead, but my muscles were no match for that taunt black cloth! I was running in slow motion! And in little bitty steps! I was a friggin' penguin!

'Arrrgggghhhhh'.

"Hey looka dat Glint—he runsa lika' slug!" exclaimed Mr. Rinaldi.

'What the hell is *he* doing here?'

"Ho, ho, ho-boy doesa' he run lika' shit!"

'Gubbidust you old fart!'

"He runsa' lika Chinesa' guy!"

'I'm running like a damn penguin!' I wanted to scream .

I was perplexed! How could this happen?!?! In front of all those people, no less! And even DOUGIE beat me! How embarrassing, particularly since his pants were halfway down by the time he finished! It wasn't much better in the 3-legged race, but I managed to eek out a trophy in the sack race event—the negative *peg factor* was minimized by keeping one's legs together and hopping. (It was also helped by Dougie falling and taking out three additional racers as he rolled around in his burlap sack.) Of course, my parents thought I was confabulating things when I arrived home with my paltry stash of trophies (1 to be exact in addition to the good sportsmanship ribbon) and blamed my miserable performance on the pants. This was evident by my father subtly winking at my mother in an all-knowing fashion as I rattled off my tale of woe. The situation was further compounded after my father later quaffed a few with Mr. Rinaldi at the local tavern, Fritz's, and my exploits were described in painful detail. Luckily, I was saved by the fact that Mr. Rinaldi said I looked like a flamingo when I was running (he had a word retrieval problem and couldn't remember 'penguin'), thereby tending to cause my father to discount the veracity of his report.

Of course, hairdos were an intricate part of the total dress gestalt—the slicker the better. Brylcreem and Vitalis were the two top choices for coiffures of distinction—one in a tube, the other in a bottle. Unfortunately, use of either lent new meaning to the term, "greaseball." This caused numerous oil slicks in local pools, defiled Little League hats, and caused difficulty sitting on Aunt Nancy's, slick, plastic-covered furniture. In fact, if one was not careful, a dangerous whiplash might occur if you plopped your head back on Aunt Nancy's couch too quickly—whoosh—yaahhhhh—there you went sliding sideways, head-first into an unsuspecting Aunt Nancy. Luckily, she was well padded, but the crucifix was potentially lethal. She typically laughed jovially, and then tweaked your cheek with a vengeance. When sitting on non-plasticized furniture one had to bend the head forward so as to not touch the back cushion, lest the tell-tale "halo" appear (it was particularly noticeable on light-colored fabrics). Some houses had these white doily things on the top of the cushions. Long visits produced numerous stiff necks, not to mention that eyeballs tended to get stuck up toward the top of the sockets.

There were two major styles—the wave or pomp (replete with a ducktail in the back) or the flattop (the front of which was augmented with Butch Wax—it *really was* a stick of wax!). The former was a three-season fashion, while the latter was typical summer fare. The flattop al-legedly kept your head cooler, although Anthony Pistillo insisted long hair was better because it absorbed the sweat. Everyone I knew, young and old, went to Johnnie's barbershop to get their haircuts. You learned quickly to go in the morning hours. This was because Johnnie would go to the back room about every 3 minutes, and then return smiling, but smelling like Barbisol or something. The more he went back there, the more he hummed. In retrospect, there was a definite cumulative effect. He also became rather intense and sometimes would mistakenly give you a flattop in the dead of winter if you weren't observant enough to scream and get him out of his "zone" before it was too late. This typically happened in the mid to late afternoon when Johnnie's eyes became red and he began to sway (Dad called it 'stagger') on his way to and from the *back room*. Once he made a wrong turn and went out the front door, leaving Philip wondering what happened—and with half a flattop. He quickly returned, however. None of us kids ever knew what was back there, although Dougie insisted Johnnie had to go to the bathroom a lot because he drank a lot of coffee and was in the war. I think Dougie's mother told him that. There also was another concoction that we used, particularly when perfecting the wave—I can't recall the name—Dell's or something—but it made your hair stiff as a board. In fact, you could skydive and not a strand would come out of place. It reminded me of Howdy Doodie's hair style and was probably as durable. Without doubt, this tonsorial addition to the overall fashion gestalt was a crowning achievement, followed later in time by Nehru jackets, madras, high-point collars, and Ben Casey/ Dr. Kildare shirts. Fairview was no slouch when it came to its own Italian designers! No, it was the zenith of style!

CHAPTER 9

A Session with Tony the Soccer Dad

"Well Tony, how has the week been?" I asked.

"Pretty good doc— we won the tournament!" Tony Piazzo replied.

"Another tournament?!?!" I asked.

"Yep—hell we hadn't had one for three weeks!"

"Oh, of course."

Poor Tony. He met the criteria for POSP—Pathologically Obsessive Sport Parent. This is a relatively new phenomenon, first noted by Benjamin Schwartz in the early 1950's when it was observed and described in a fledgling form at local neighborhood Little League fields. Since then, it has enjoyed a meteoric, geometric progression, expanding to sports such as gymnastics, soccer, swimming, football, dirt bike racing, and ping-pong. Apparently track has remained immune to this disorder, as most POSPs tend to shy away from track shorts and cannot give unsolicited pointers on how to jump hurdles, pole vault, or do a running broad jump. (Notwithstanding the fact that most POSPs couldn't hit a baseball, kick a soccer ball, or swim more than 12 yards—nor could they have done it in their prime). Plus, they become bored, because at track meets the repertoire of what they can yell during an event was severely limited to "Run!" "Go!"or "Faster."

"Run, run, run!"

"Go, go, go!"

"Faster, faster!" or, more creatively:

"Run, faster, run, go go, faster, faster, GO! Run!" Other sports obviously provided infinitely more creative combinations.

Tony is a bona-fide, card carrying, Soccer POSP. This breed is characterized by demonstrating at least 8 of the following symptoms for more than 12 months with no more than 24 hours of symptom-free behavior: 1) absence from home most weekends from Valentine's Day to Thanksgiving (January 1st to December 31st in warmer climates); 2) distinct attitude that his/her kid is the best, key, primo, impact player on the team; 3) conviction that his/her kid doesn't have enough playing time and that the coach knows squat; 4) recurrent nightmares that the son (or daughter) would lose the ability to kick a ball if they did not play soccer for more than one week; 5) compulsion to have kid play Fall ball, Indoor Winter soccer, Spring Soccer, and the summer tournament circuit (leaving a total of 6 days in August without soccer); 6) Unflagging belief that his/her kid will go to a Division I college on a full-ride soccer scholarship and then on to the World Cup; 7) Delusion that he/she actually know the rules of soccer; 8) frequent spectator rage, as evident by screaming at own team, opposing team, referees, linesmen, opposing parents, small pets, concession workers, the sky, etc.; 9) compulsion to drink large quantities of beer at away games, beginning at 8:00 a.m. and culminating at 3:00 a.m. the next morning, 11) total inability to play soccer himself/herself; and 12) owns a minivan or SUV with a soccer ball sticker emblazoned with the team name and the kid's number displayed prominently on the rear window.

Poor Tony met 12/12 criteria, making the diagnosis relatively easy. Like most POSPs, Tony began to show prodromal symptoms quite early. In Tony's case, it began when his son, Jay, turned four. I recall Tony's wife, Emma, (who also has POSP—which, incidentally, makes the prognosis for recovery for either of them about nil—folie a deux they call it) recounting a story when Jay was playing K-division YMCA soccer. Apparently, Jay, who thus far had been clueless about the game, actually finally tried to kick a ball out of the beehive formation, missed, but fell on the ball causing to lazily roll 5 feet and knock over one of the cones that defined the goal. The Ref said, "no goal," the onlookers said "ooohhhh," and Tony began a non-stop, vociferous, monologue about the Ref's heritage (something about his mother), done while vigorously jumping up and down, flailing his arms, and turning very red. This was verified by a bootleg videotape taken by another parent and submitted to America's Funniest Home Videos. There are rumored sightings on U-tube as well. Everyone else, including the beehive of 4-year olds stood motionless, totally quiet, and watched in amazement this unbridled display of temper prowess. Tony finally sputtered out of energy and was sweating profusely, wheezing heavily and almost fell to his knees, but he was immediately reinvigorated when the Ref produced a red card (meaning you're outta' here, bucko). He again launched into a vigorous display, but this could by no means match the intensity, grace, creativity, or duration of the first attempt. The Ref suspended the game, and the kids, including Jay, were eager to go to the Treat Mom to get Twinkies and Kool Aid, not exactly knowing (or caring) who won. However, that red card was a milestone and the first in a long line for Tony—to him, a veritable red badge of courage!

"So, how did *you* do in the tournament?" I queried.

"Pretty good."

"*Pretty* good?"

"Yeah, I left quietly after I got the red card, but I went up on top of the hill to watch."

"Anything else?"

"Well….I broke another lawn chair."

His eighth of the season.

"How?"

"I threw it on the field—I was trying to hit this loudmouth on the other sideline, but I got the linesman instead."

"You got the linesman instead?!?" I asked incredulously.

"The guy yelled at me to shut up and he said we sucked! I told him to bring his sorry ass over here and I'd kick it for him."

At that point I had a vision of two sumos charging at each other across the field of battle, oblivious to everything outside of the intensely focused tunnel vision centered on the soon-to-be-vanquished opponent. The sumo analogy was particularly poignant since Tony was moustachioed, of medium height, wider girth, balding but combing his hair from his left ear over the top to the right ear, bow legged and sporting belly padding ample to meet another gut charging head on.

"I started going across the field and he started coming too."

'Gunfight at the OK Corral.' I mused.

"What were the kids doing?" I asked.

"First they just ran around us, then they all started yelling at each other and the game stopped."

"Other parents?"

"They all started yelling too! The Ref gave me and that jerk red cards and said if everyone didn't shut up, the game was over—I guess since it was a 1-1 tie everyone shut up."

"You?"

"Well I sorta' yelled some stuff from up on the hill, but I don't think they could hear me."

'Exemplary sportsmanship,' I mused.

"Tony, this isn't good for you—neither your mental or your physical health! You may need to take Zoloft or some other SSRI!"

"Can I drink beer if I'm on the medicine?"

"Not recommended."

"No meds for me—besides I have a tournament next week."

"Where at?"

"Cincinnati-4th of July Firecracker Kickoff—actually Jay will be at soccer camp but the wife and I are going anyway—there's nothing else to do."

Nothing like stay home, cook hotdogs on the grill, and socialize with the neighbors or anything. This wasn't the first time for this kind of behavior. Tony has been observed aimlessly wandering soccer fields on Sunday afternoons when Jay wasn't playing, honing his spectator skills and displays of undefatiguable frenzy at the expense of unsuspecting teams and innocent referees. He also went to every soccer game held at the three local colleges, typically loitered at the local soccer shop, and put his name on every soccer camp mailing list. He went so far as to let Jay wear a soccer haircut—a sort of mullet with a rat-tail, bleached tips, and his number shaved on the sides. This was a step above many of the coiffures noted on the field of play—a good number of which looked as if they were done by a barber who was farsighted and on LSD (or Johnnie at the end of a long day of trips to the back room).

Tony was suspected of having Seasonal Affective Disorder (SAD), but I think it had nothing to do with light—he was just in tournament withdrawal. This may explain his attempts to have the team play soccer in indoor Christmas and New Years' tournaments. Even some of the diehard POSPs paled at the prospect, particularly since the games were three and one half hours away, and the likelihood of snow during transit was great. Besides, most other (non-PSOP symptomatic) family members tended to not be sympathetic with such decisions.

The session went on, with Tony underscoring minor victories in his battle with POSP syndrome. These were *very* minor victories. He did cut a dashing figure in his bright red Kicksters (Name of Jay's team) t-shirt, hat, and warm up jacket. The latest trophy tucked under his right arm was quite the conversation piece as well—I'm sure he was screaming inside for someone to ask an innocent question about it, affording Tony the opportunity to launch into a well-rehearsed soliloquy. I thought better of taking him up on the subtle invitation.

"See you next week, doc."

"Okay Tony, but don't lose it again in Cincinnati."

"Hell, Jay isn't even playing, so I won't get excited."

'And I'm the King of Prussia.'

Tony strolled out and I overheard Connie make the dreadful mistake of asking him about the trophy —alas…

I sat back, the trophy discussion droning on outside my door, and mused about the sports scene when I was growing up.....hell we never even heard of soccer......but we had Little League!

CHAPTER 10
Youth Sports in Fairview

Fairview was not a hotbed for team athletics. Maybe that was because there was no high school, with students being sent to a neighboring town for their higher education. But one thing that was *really* big was Little League baseball! From age four onward every kid dreamed of playing in *The Majors*. It was almost as good as playing in the Rough Riders Drum and Bugle Corps (which, incidentally, played Moon Over Miami much better than the school safety patrol—more later).

In fact, Mr. Rinaldi could often be heard encouraging the youngsters of baseball-playing age who were trying out their newly acquired Italian cuss words, "You bedda' be good o' you no playa' da' basa' ball onna' da' Coop (Italian) team! I seea' to that!"

There were several premier teams that had long-held baseball dynasties: the Battaglias (black hats and socks), the Italian Cooperative (aka "Coop," with green hats and socks), the Cigolini's (maroon attire) and the VFW (spiffy blue apparel). There were other, less desired teams such as Southern Trucking (red theme). The progression was that you typically started off in the Minors, but you could go straight to the Majors if: a) you were *really* good; b) your father routinely drank beer with the coach (some said it was even better if your *mother* drank beer with the coach); or c) you developed a reputation with the other kids as being "cool." Everyone made it to the Majors eventually, although some kids were so bad they'd stay in the Minors for three years and then make it to the big time for year four just because it was a rule (they'd usually play left field after the team was leading by at least 23 runs). In Fairview, baseball prowess was therefore measured by the yardstick of how quickly you got to the Majors. A meteoric rise indicated superb skill (or a beer-drinking mother). Getting there by year four was a sign of mediocrity (accompanied by persistence).

I originally was on the VFW Minor league team. I tried pitching. I was sure that speed and not necessarily accuracy was the key to impressing the coach and other players. My hopes for a career at this position were quickly dashed when a blazing fastball careened into the dugout and bopped Coach Ginnanoni (many names ended in "i") on the back of his head (at least it bounced once before it hit him). To make matters worse, he had a new hat on and the bounce in the wet dirt caused the ball to leave a perfect, reddish brown circle on the back of his spiffy, white and blue hat—and that dirt *never* came out of *anything*! I think they sprayed oil on the dirt but no one ever saw a truck or anything—oil slicks were reported to occur when washing uniforms and no grass grew on that field—not even weeds! Very peculiar in retrospect, particularly since this urban moonscape also included the outfield. It also became increasingly difficult to conscript someone to catch for me, this most likely associated with the frequent need to keep climbing over the fence to retrieve the ball after a pitch that was blazing in speed, but sorely lacking in accuracy. I then was moved (rather abruptly) to second base. I did fairly well there until I crashed into the shortstop while both of us were going after a pop-up fly. Unfortunately, I knocked the shortstop, Joey's, tooth out *and* I dropped the ball. Even more unfortunate was the fact that Joey was the coach's son and the dropped ball allowed the winning run to score. Bad karma and the first of many indicators that a career in baseball was not in the cards.

I was then moved to third base (and told to stay away from Joey). My tenure in that position was short-lived and I could directly tie the reason into a particular event. We were winning 2 to 1 against Southern Trucking, and it was the bottom of the ninth, with bases loaded. Pete Petrone (aka Moose) blasted a grounder at me—oohh boy, not good! It was a two-hopper, but the ball went over my glove and hit me right, square in the gut, with a resounding thud. There I was writhing in that purportedly oil-tinged reddish brown dirt, trying to say something, but all that came out was something like "gurrgghhh" or "gaaaccckkk." I was even trying to muster up some of Dougie's favorite f-bombs, but they were stuck somewhere between my belly button and Adam's apple. The red-hatted (and socked) players had absolutely no empathy—everyone simply ran past or jumped over me on their way to home plate. All I saw was a blur of crimson! Joey kept yelling at me to roll over so he could get the ball.

"Glint—move outta' there—give me the friggin' ball!"

"Gurrgghhh."

"Glint, MOVE!!"

"Gaaaccckkk. Waahhhh."

I remember gazing over at the dugout. The coach's eyes were bugging out of his head like he had on really pegged pants or something, and he was *really* red, his mouth was moving like crazy, but I couldn't make out what he was saying. The assistant coach was stomping up and down. He was hatless, having tossed his hat in the dirt, totally disregarding the oil hazard. The rest of the team was staring like they were in shock. I heard a voice that was distinct from the others:

"Glint—getta' da' ball now—getta' up offa' you ass!"

It was Mr. Rinaldi! What was he doing there?!? God, the pinnacle of embarrassment! Not to mention the play by play that would follow at Fritz's—replete with word substitutions!

Pete tripped over me and he went face first toward third base. By that time Joey had finally gotten the ball out from under me and tagged him out. At least I prevented a grand slam. Unfortunately the coach was not as impressed, and my next position was dreaded left field. Banished! That was to be my terminal position for the rest of my illustrious Little League career.

I stayed in that position even in the Majors. Once, however, while in left field I made the play of the summer. THE play of my baseball career! Jack Wienstein, a local ruffian, who also was the clean up man for the Coop (green apparel) whacked the snot out of a pitch thrown by Warren "fastball" Dudge. I was gazing at the interesting advertisements on the left field fence when I was alerted by a distinct 'crack,' the roar of the crowd, and the blood curdling screams of my coach. I turned to see the ball hurling at me like a rocket. I started backpeddling like crazy with blazing speed (luckily my baseball pants weren't pegged) and jumped in desperation with every ounce of strength that I had (enhanced by raw fear). I heard the crowd roaring as I landed and was shocked to see half the ball protruding from the web of my glove. All the base-runners, assuming this was a thumbs down home run, had to turn around and run back the other way. I was so excited I fired the ball to the infield, but, unfortunately, it bopped the kid running back from third to second base—but Joey caught it off the kid's head and then tagged him (not too difficult since the kid was sort of standing there holding his head) and then threw it to first but they already had one out and the first baseman was walking away. The coach was bopped again when the ball flew into the dugout, almost in the exact same spot as before (he was turned congratulating the assistant coach). I didn't see if it left another round mark. Unfortunately, my father missed the play. He went to the bathroom as he thought it was going to be my turn at bat soon and he wanted to spare himself the pain of watching the product of his loins tarnish the Wayward name by another fruitless experience at home plate.

Yes, batting was a similar fiasco. The bats ranged from a size 28 to a 34 or something. Bigger kids used bigger bats. Smaller, skinny kids who wanted to be cool also used bigger bats, though much less efficiently. I fell into the latter category. Big bats were also *heavy*—as physics would have it—and little muscles + big, heavy, object = very slow swing (usually after the ball had passed). My clever strategy was to draw a walk as frequently as possible. To do so I would crunch up into a fetal ball-like position in an attempt to reduce the strike zone to the size of a postage stamp.

"Steeee-rike one!"

Scrunch up a bit more.

"Steeee-rike two!"

Damn, really scrunch up now.

"Steee-rike three—you're out!"

'How in the hell did he get that ball in the strike zone?—I was exquisitely scrunched!' I would repeatedly ask myself. If I did swing I would have to start as soon as the pitcher got ready to let go of the ball so as to afford me enough time to get the bat around (because I held it really far back in my patented scrunch stance). Unfortunately, I had to guess where the ball was going. I didn't typically guess well. To make matters worse, the weight of the bat and the effort I gave sometimes caused me go out of control and look like a helicopter or a rendition of Mr. Stannoni's swing-in-a-circle-with-the-cane, as I spun wildly off toward the dugout—striking fear in the hearts of my teammates that I would flail in there at them, whacking to the left and then to the right, in a totally indiscriminant fashion. A veritable bat-wielding, whirling dervish!

Once I was at bat and the announcers in the elevated booth right up behind home plate forgot to turn off the mike.

"He has *how many* strike-outs?" said one voice.

"Wow, that many! Friggin' unbelievable!" said another.

"Steee-rike three—you're out!" blared the umpire.

'Damn, just improved the record!' I thought to myself.

It got to the point that I resorted to telling family members the wrong times for the games. They resorted to making believe they misunderstood the time that I told them. As a result, occasionally, my wrong time and their "misunderstanding" coincided, and they actually showed up at the game by mistake. I always worried that they would resort to wearing Groucho Marx disguises to remain anonymous as they sat in the bleachers—or at least really dark sunglasses or bags over their heads with eye-holes cut out. My mother was the eternal optimist, saying such things as:

"You almost hit it on that second spin around.", or "That scrunch was excellent," "Good walk!" or "Your uniform looks really nice," or "I'll say a rosary for you." Good ol' mom. Dad was less empathic and more to the point: "Glint that *really* sucked!" or "What the hell do you call that? Or, "Maybe it was the mailman."

Every now and then I became exceptionally lucky and really got hold of a pitch. Usually the hit went to right field (due to the fact that I was just launching the swing-of- the-whirling-dervish by the time the ball was going by). Once I even got a triple, but the game was called in the third inning because of lightening and the other team protested or something and as a result, it didn't count (I was absolutely certain that towering shot silenced those announcers and left them in awe!).

Sometimes, to save face I think, the coach would send us to be a baseline coach. You were supposed to stay in this rectangular box by first or third base and tell the runners whether they should advance or stay put. You could also covertly rub the reddish dirt on your uniform to make it look like you actually did something during the game. The only problem was that the runners never listened to you (perhaps because the less than skilled players were usually the 'coach du jour' in the boxes). So the trick was to yell and point in the direction that the kid was going—if it looked like he wasn't slowing down, you simply screamed for him to go. Conversely, if it looked like he *was* slowing down, you yelled for him to stop. The spectators were easily duped—but probably didn't give a hoot as to what the fools in the boxes were doing anyway. Unfortunately, Paulie never did get the technique down, and he sometimes screamed to the base-runner to keep going, even though the kid had just drawn a walk.

Another favorite youth sport pastime was dodgeball, which was played during Mr. Sarubbie's summer camp on the baseball field in a large, lined rectangle (typically drawn in the grassless left-center field area). The object of the game was to soundly hit as many opposing players with the ball as possible, without them catching it. Two groups of kids would stand on opposing sides, wailing the volleyball as hard as possible at each other. If you were hit, you went to "prison"—which was a sort of time-out place behind the opposing team. If you threw a ball and had the misfortune of someone catching it, you'd go to prison too. That situation was useful in that you and your teammates who were in prison could throw the ball back and forth, with the opponents running around like idiots between you, not knowing whether the player on the field or the one in prison was going to try to hit them. This situation was particularly unnerving for anxiety-prone players. You would try to aim at the head or legs, because it was hard to catch the ball in those areas; if you hit the kid in the stomach, he might fold over and actually catch it. The groin was okay too, in fact, Mary, the only girl player and something of a tomboy, was notorious for the legendary "groin cruncher" tosses. She seemed to take great delight in having writhing boys flopping around like tuna in the reddish dust in front of her. Later I would find out that Freud labeled this 'penis envy.' Little did she know that most of us would writhe on the ground even if the ball hit remotely close to the "spot," this in an effort to make others think that we had ample assets of manhood, even at these early ages (particularly since we covertly thought that Mary was kind of cute, even though publically all of us swore she had cooties). Once Paulie took it a bit too far and began holding his crotch and writhing after he got hit in the nose. Paulie got confused easily.

Everyone would try to get Steve Armato on their side—he had good hands, was a good ducker, and he could throw the ball like a rocket. He *never* went to prison, either. If he was already on the other side, you'd try to get Mary, even though you wouldn't want to admit it. Warren Dudge was another excellent choice—he was the fastest kid around and he could dart, roll, jump, contort (even better than my at-bat stances), duck, *and* catch. The only drawback was, as mentioned previously, that Warren typically would say "wooo, wooo, wooo" when he ran (probably too much Three Stooges, we speculated). This was a definite detractor from his credibility, but nonetheless made it great sport to watch.

We had this one premier, sure to go down in history, game-of-games, where Mary was in prison, Steve was her teammate, and Warren was our only guy left, running back and forth in between them. The game went on forever. Mr. Sarubbie took the ball back because camp was closing for the day, so Steve used his basketball. Just the two of them left (with Mary lurking in prison). Steve fired the basketball like it was exiting from a cannon, Warren, wooo, wooo, woooing all over the place. In fact, most of the kids in prison went home for dinner, leaving the diehard holdouts to watch this test of wills go on into dusk.

"Take this—urrrggghh!" and the ball would fly.

"Wooo, wooo, wooo," and Warren scampered out of harm's way.

"Urrrggghhh!" again.

"Wooo, wooo, wooo!"

"Urrrggghhh!"

"Wooo, wooo, wooo!"

The scene took on a mesmerizing quality, sort of like watching a Wimbleton tennis match, but with different sound effects and a skinny kid running side to side like a ping-pong ball. The cadence was such that the onlookers in prison tended to get drowsy, and this caused Dougie to get a bloody nose, as he stood there after hearing numerous "urrrggghhh's" and the "wooo, wooo, wooo's," but not realizing that Warren had sidestepped the bullet of a throw and the new target was now his face.

"Urrrggghhh!"

"Wooo, wooo, wooo!"

"Pow!"

"Aaacckkk—f**kkkkkk…Thud."

"Oohhhh!" said the remaining crowd in unison.

Dougie was unusually quiet. Didn't even mutter any more F-words!

Seasoned dodgeball veterans often used clever tactics. These included: 1) get some of the fat, slow kids on your side—they were good targets and you could also hide behind them— an added bonus was that they sometimes actually caught the ball; 2) encourage other players to taunt the kid with the ball, thereby drawing attention away from you (Paulie typically could be persuaded to do this); 3) *Never* go "wooo, wooo, wooo"!; 4) Try to mingle with the kids in prison so as to confuse their teammates who were still in the game; and 5) *Never* jump straight up in the air, as the likelihood of jumping completely over the oncoming ball was infinitely small, while the likelihood of getting hit in the assets was extraordinarily high (with bona fide, justifiable writhing to boot).

Paulie, in a flash of brilliance, once tried putting glue on his hands so as to catch the ball better. He used Tester's model airplane glue. First his hands were really sticky (which didn't help when he got hit in the face), then they got dirty and sticky, and then they got just dirty. No one wanted Paulie to touch the ball, because he kept leaving dirty, moderately sticky handprints on it. Paulie's eyes took on a glazed reddish appearance—perhaps a consequence of putting his face too close to the glue's fumes for a period of time. Then the glue dried and Paulie was left with really dirty hands that wouldn't come clean when he washed them. He looked like he was wearing reddish-brown gloves for the next week! Not to mention that he smelled like a Monogram 1/24th scale car model. Plus, everyone usually tried to hit Paulie in the head anyway.

Youth sports were not restricted to the baseball park, though. There were several other recreational opportunities. For example, the town fathers took great pride in providing discount tickets for us to go to the "World's Largest Outdoor Saltwater Pool" at Palisades Amusement Park. The Fairviewite parents were delighted that the kids were afforded the opportunity to engage in water sports at the bargain price of 40 cents per day. It was the mayor's election year motto that 'every kid has a pool' or something like that. What the town fathers didn't tell the parents or kids, however, was the fact that two times per week the so-called salt water was pumped up from the Hudson River. Coincidentally, this occurred on the very same days the Fairview kids had their pool excursions. The Hudson River was polluted as hell—the water was brackish, green, cold, and definitely salty. It also had unidentifiable objects floating in the mix. Some effluent came down pipes along the Palisades and just emptied into the river, and other pipes would pump it right back up—to the pool with the Fairview kids bobbing around in it, their heads looking like dark beans in some kind of green soup. Heavy metals, light metals, e-coli, PCBs, salt, chlorine, Krypton, and other exotic ingredients, all stirred up into a primordial, frothy brew by the thrashing kids from Fairview. In fact, the only fish that lived in the river were eels. We used to catch them in the mud in a town called Edgewater (which, coincidentally, was on the edge of the water of the Hudson River—again attesting to the keen perceptiveness of the town fathers), by the rotting barges. Dougie said that his brother caught an eel with two heads. We believed Dougie, but Philip didn't. If you threw a rock in the mud, one would hear a distinct 'plup' and then it was gone—just like that! Dougie said if you walked out there it was like quicksand and that there were hundreds of skeletons deep down in the mud.

Generally believing Dougie, we nonetheless once tried to test that hypothesis. We voted that Paulie should go out there (after all he *was* the tallest) and the rest of us would hold on to him with a rope. Lo and behold, Paulie only sank up to his waist, but it took us forever to get him out of there. Paulie kept crying and whining that he couldn't move his legs and that he was going to die when the tide came in. That was pretty perceptive of Paulie—in fact—it was something we had totally overlooked! He calmed down when I convinced him that he would float right out of the mud when the water level rose (it *was* salt water after all!). After what seemed like ten hours, we got Paulie out of that muck, but he smelled really bad. We made him walk way behind us. He must have gotten close to one of those down-hill pipes or something. Rumor had it that his mother chased him out of his house with a broom and made him take off his shoes, socks, and pants and throw them in the garbage can—right on Fairview Avenue in front of buses and everything (across from Little Al's). We didn't notice it at the time, but Paulie also lost one of his size 13 shoes—this would cause quite a problem because Little Al had limited access to such grand sizes for his Shoe Corner!

We decided to go to the pool for the first time on a Monday, caught the #22 bus, and tooled on up to Palisades Park (often called Walisades by our Hispanic visitors). Because we arrived at around 10 in the morning, nothing much was going on—the carnies who worked there (who we heard so much about and were sternly instructed to avoid at all costs because they kidnapped and ate kids) must have been asleep somewhere.

Philip and his friends had given us the scoop on the place. After you came out of the reeking, salty-smelling locker room, you were supposed to head to the 'boards'—*not* the far beach (sand). No one wanted to go to the "beach" because there were millions of little kids with tubes on running around, plus you had to walk for a 100 yards at least before the water became deep—not to mention there were these little waves. Plus it was heavily seeded with cigarette butts and other mysterious buried things. Since we were at the height of discovering our manhood assets, the slow walk into the frigid water could become a real test of one's mettle, particularly as it reached the fabled CCH (critical crotch height).

Wesley, Ritchie, Skaris and Ritchie's cousin, Arthur, and I strolled to the boards and put our towels down. They ran over to the rope that spanned the deep end of the pool and jumped right in. Unfortunately, I hadn't learned to swim yet due to the fact that swimming was very hard to master in the foot-deep wading pool that we had in our yard (even though Philip swears that he perfected his breast stroke there). So I deferred and walked down the boards a bit to a point where '4 feet' was written on the side of the pool in red. The rest of the gang came down and watched me jump in.

"Yahoo!" I yelled as I brazenly jumped in and immediately began my extremely rapid descent into the brackish depths.

'Four feet my ass!' I immediately thought, 'I'm friggin' drowning!'

"Glub, glub, glub," I gurgled.

I began kicking and flailing like crazy and popped my head out of the water for approximately 500 msec.

"Glint—you okay?" Richie yelled.

'Gaack, glub, gaack," I replied as I submerged once again.

As I sank into the quiet depths, I looked up and saw distorted faces peering down at me from over the edge of the pool. Their mouths were moving and they were waving their arms. All I could hear was bubbles—MY bubbles!

'What a way to go!' I thought. 'Drowned in Walisades Amusement Park pool! My friends looking at me like I was a sinker in a polluted fishbowl!'

'Four feet my ass!'

Then I saw it—the ladder was almost right next to me. Sweet Jesus! Rather than try to go straight up, I went sideways, using every movable part of my body in crablike desperation, and some way, somehow, I got a grip on the bottom run and pulled like hell. By about that time, Arthur grabbed my hand and gave me a heave-ho.

"Gaack, what the hell…glub, cough, gasp!" I blurted.

A lifeguard, who had been talking to two girls with sizable assets and very small bathing suits, twirled his whistle, sauntered over, and suggested I might think about swimming in shallower water.

'*Swim!*' I thought, 'You call *that* swimming? I think of it more like *sinking*! F***ing sinking at that! Four feet my ass! I was at the bottom and there still was two feet of water above me!'

I meekly crawled up the ladder and immediately began to experience the worst pounding headache imaginable. I was thinking about the hammer and anvil in the Excedrin commercials and was sure it was a sledge hammer in this case. I staggered over to the towels and, for all intensive purposes, passed out. Unfortunately, instead of suntan lotion, Philip told us to use baby oil with iodine for a *really good tan!* I had put some on in the locker room and even though I left an oil slick at the scene of the alleged *swim*, I still must have had some on. I was definitely white as a ghost by most standards (another drawback of the wading pool was that it was under huge pear trees), the paleness undoubtedly intensified by the very recent, near-death experience. Needless to say after a while I felt that I might be getting too tanned, so I flipped over, slathered more baby oil on, and again drifted off, not hearing Wesley admonish me for using such primitive means of tanning. Wesley, replete with red hair and at least one million freckles, was on the cutting edge of tanning—QT— short for *Quick Tan*. With this stuff, you could tan in the basement, because it somehow stained your skin or something. Unfortunately, about an hour or two after he QT'd, he began to turn orange—even the palms of his hands took on a pumpkinesque hue. Wesley looked like some type of squash with glasses. We overhead some of the Puerto Rican kids (who didn't worry too much about tanning) say things like:

"Hey man, you see 'dat keed over there? He looks fuuunnny!"

"Hey looks like a beeg cheeze doodle!"

"Nahh, man, he looks like f***ing carrotman or somethin'!—he must glow in the dark!"

We felt very sorry for Wesley, about his not securing the proper bronze look or anything.

"Yaaaaahhhhh!" was my response when we hit the showers (everyone showered with their bathing suit on allegedly because we wanted to wash the salt out—insisting it had nothing to do with 'shrivies').

"Gee Glint, you look pretty red," mused Skaris.

"Glint, you look like a beet head!" echoed Ritchie, "man your ass is really white!" (after I strategically slipped the suit down to suprapubic latitude).

"Look at dat.!—another one with fuuuunnny colors," said one of the Hispanics. "Cheeze Doodle's friend looks like a tomato wit a white ass!"

After getting dressed, I felt the heat radiating through my t-shirt, sort of like some thermonuclear rays or something. I thought I was melting. It got worse on the bus ride home to the point that I was convinced that I, too, would glow once the sun went down. I had to sit straight up so my back wouldn't touch the seat. Here we were, the glow brothers: tomato head and his sidekick, cheese doodle.

"Mom! Glint looks like a beethead!" bellowed Philip in a less than empathic manner as soon as I came to the door.

"Glint what *did* you do?" Mom chimed in after being alerted to my dire condition by my dearest brother who unfortunately had not yet become a priest.

"I was lying on the boards and I got a little sunburned," I responded, while Philip amused himself by leaving various white handprints on my scarlet, still-sizzling, flesh.

Two days later, Ritchie, Arthur, Skaris and I (now fondly deemed the King of Noxema or Son of Solarcaine, or Tomato Head) all visited

Dr. Dannon because of earaches—the dreaded *Walisades Swimmer's Ear!* The kids of Fairview made Dr. Dannon a wealthy man during the summer months by presenting with epidemics of swimmer's ear caused by microbes floating in the primordial, salt water soup.

Unfortunately, despite intensive training and opportunity, to my knowledge no kid from Fairview ever made it to the Olympics or the professional leagues in swimming, baseball, or dodgeball. However, they did develop a healthy fear of carnies and a resistance to the hoards of exotic microbes and other things that dwelled in those murky, mysterious waters of the World's Largest Saltwater Pool!

CHAPTER 11

A session on Discipline

"He's a little monster! He's bipolar!! He's possessed!" wailed Michelle Edsel, a 30-something, single mom who brought her son, Hudson, in for an evaluation at the *strong* urging of his preschool teachers.

"How old is Hudson?" I queried. I also thought his parents got too carried away with this car-theme thing....Hudson Edsel...what's his middle name, Ford?

"Four—but he thinks he's an adult—like he's equal to me!"

"Adult? How do you know that?"

"Because he says so—says he's the boss and he doesn't have to listen to me."

"What do you do when he says that?"

"I explain to him that I've the mommy and he's the little boy and he hurts my feelings," she sobbed.

"His response?" I asked.

"He tells me to shut up—and I cry like a little girl!" she moaned.

"Oh, a bit contrary is he?" I replied.

"A BIT?!? He doesn't listen to anyone! He HITS me! He treats me like I'M the kid! He called his teacher the B-word loud enough for her to hear when she told him to sit down for circle time! He urinated on the monkey bars at recess!"

I was rapidly forming an opinion about Hudson, but this was a no-no, since I hadn't even seen him yet. Heck, even the bagger at Shop and Save could make a pretty good guess on this one!

"What disciplinary techniques have you tried?" I asked.

"EVERYTHING!!" was the reply. Aha! First rule in the diagnosis of ineffective parenting—if they said they tried everything, then they didn't do *anything* correctly. A clinical pearl, gleaned over the years of vast experience. I was self-amazed with the incisiveness of my clinical acumen! 'Keep going Glint!' I cheered to myself.

"Like what?"

"Time-outs, ignoring, explaining, spanking, soap in his mouth, telling him Mommy is terribly disappointed, hiding in the closet. Nothing works—even taking his favorite blankie away from him at night!"

"Time-outs, if administered properly, usually work," I lectured in a perhaps too dogmatic fashion.

"He won't stay in time out!" Michelle wailed. "I put him in the chair—he gets up. I put him back there and he gets up again. I hold him there—he screams and kicks. He spits! He hits me! He says he hates me and he's going to chop my head off with a machete!"

'Wow, really out of control. This could be more serious that the run of the mill terrible 4's'I thought (they follow the terrible 3's which come after the terrible 2's and continue upwards until the terrible 20's).

She continued, "I send him to his room and he empties the drawers, rips his sheets off the bed, and throws things all over the place! Calling me a doo-doo head all the while!"

"How long has this been going on?" I asked.

"Since he's been able to walk! The doo-doo head since he was able to talk! He's been kicked out of 5 daycares and preschools and he's working on number 6! His grandparents refuse to watch him—they keep saying they're going to the Ozarks every time I ask them to babysit. Hell, they can't be going to the Ozarks that much! Who goes to the Ozarks in February?!"

"Do you use other babysitters?" I ventured.

"Not anymore! He mooned one, called 911 on another, locked himself in the bathroom for 2 hours for the next to last one (repeatedly flushing the toilet), and most recently locked the last girl out of the house after coaxing her out on the front porch saying the pizza guy was there (even though she didn't order pizza)! She had to climb in a back window—wrecked the screen too. Plus she sprained her ankle in the process!"

Ms. Edsel was obviously at the end of her proverbial rope—abandoned by any allies—left alone to face the wrath of 4-year-old Hudson (The Masher) Edsel, one-on-one. I pitied the poor woman!

Eureka! I thought of potential reinforcements! "Is Dad in the picture?" I asked hopefully.

"We're divorced. He makes occasional cameo appearances. He says Hudson is all boy and it's my fault he doesn't listen and that he never has a problem. That's because they always play videogames when they are together. And it isn't Star Wars Leggo's that they play—Call of Duty, Halo—that kind of stuff! Besides, he hasn't seen Hudson for 6 weeks!" Her eyes were bulging and her neck was red as a beet.

"Let me meet with Hudson for a bit," I suggested. This was a very timely statement, particularly since he again was opening the door uninvited for the 8th time in the last 10 minutes. He was frowning and complaining that the waiting room toys were for babies. Obviously he had not discovered the latest copy of Esquire with the 'women we love' feature. Since he had already entered the room, I took the initiative and invited him to have a seat, stating that it's Mom's turn to wait outside.

"No-she stays! Sit down!" was his order to his Mom.

"The Doctor said that mommy needs to play with the toys now, okay?" she pleaded meekly.

"You don't play with baby toys! Stay here!" was the Atilla-the-tyke's terse reply.

Pretty darn authoritative for what I sized up to be a 32 inch, 35 pound, tow-headed munchkin in sweat pants and a sweatshirt fittingly emblazoned with "Mommy's Little Terror." He must have been eating spaghetti for lunch too.

"Rules are rules and Moms and kids take turns and now it's your turn." I said with an ample amount of authority. Mom slinked out, whereupon Hudson sat sideways in the chair, folded his hands behind his head and said:

"So what do you want to ask me?"

'Amazing—a breakthrough already. Still have that old touch, Wayward!' I mused, stifling a wry smile. "How about we start with why you think you're here today?"

"Don't know. Don't want to be here and I don't want to talk to you!" was the brisk reply.

'Kiddie omerta!'

Parrying, I said, "Mom said you got in trouble in preschool."

"I don't want to talk about that!" he said as I now stared at the back of his head. Very effective way of breaking eye contact—right to the point.

"What did you do?" I asked.

"Broke rules 1 and 4 but I don't want to tell you about that!"

"Of course you don't have to tell me what you did—just tell me what rules 1 and 4 are," I smoothly proposed, basking in my self-ordained cleverness.

"Rule number 1—listen to the teacher. Rule number 4—keep your hands, feet and objects to yourself," was the matter-of-fact reply.

'Definitely oppositional.' "What happens if you break one of those rules?"

"You get a red card and you go to the *red chair* and when you get three red cards it's the *red chair* and you go to the *principal's office* too! I always have to go there."

This was a private preschool through high school operation, notorious for the indiscriminant use of RED CHAIR! It has been effectively employed to break the will of legions of rambunctious preschoolers over the years—But this nemesis of the misbehaved was no deterrent for Hudson!

"Then what happens?" I questioned.

"The principal calls mommy and tells her I have to go home."

'Now he's Mom's problem—pretty clever principal!'

I noticed that Hudson was becoming increasingly fidgety, this more evident as I gazed at him lying on the floor, hands behind his head, looking at the overhead lights whimsically. That lasted 4.5 seconds, whereupon he was looking out the window, then pacing up and down the room, then under the table, this interspersed with periodic feints of bolting toward the door. No matter what question I posed to Hudson, he started to answer but then was sidetracked within 3.2 seconds. He fell out of his chair a total of 11 times, giving me an idea for a quick money maker—velcro seat straps for interview chairs! He often found great delight in dashing to the light switch and turning the overheads off. Little did he know I was a veteran of such antics in the past and that is why I now have a room with windows. In my previous office that was not the case and switching off the light had a greater impact, this typically followed by adults blindly crashing about the room in an attempt to turn the lights on once again. After several such occurrences I resorted to concealing a flashlight in a drawer that could be easily retrieved in total darkness at a moment's notice.

My interview with Hudson was not going well by any standard, necessitating yet another change in tactics.

"I have an idea there buddy boy—I'm going to work with Mom and come up with a program where you get PRIZES! But only if you're a good boy in school!"

"I don't want to be a good boy in school to get stupid prizes!" was the terse reply.

'This calls for yet another change in tactics—plan C!' This kid was tough!

"And if you're *not* good there are going to be *consequences!*" (This said to at least confuse him with the big word because it sounds important and he has no idea what it means!—again, those years of experience pay off!).

"I don't want consenences!"

Sensing vulnerability, I moved in for the kill: "Consequences like no TV, no computer, no Bionicals, and no going outside to play!" I sneered.

"Not the Bionicals!!" he screamed.

"No problem!" I replied, "Just follow rule 1 and 4 at school and it's no consequences and a trip to the Treasure Chest."

"I don't want to play with the baby toys in the waiting room!" he said in a clever maneuver to switch the topic.

"Leggos aren't baby toys."

"Are too!"

"Are not!"

"Are too!"

'Wait! What am I doing here?! Whatever it is, I'm losing! That kid's going to be a lawyer!' Hudson was briskly "escorted" out of the room while his mom came back in, the door closing in a flash.

"I think it best that we focus on preschool—more specifically, keeping him in it. Let's pick rules 1 and 4: if he complies with them he gets a reward at home. If he messes up, no reward and there will be consequences. A grab bag for good behavior and losing stuff like TV or Bionicals if the behavior isn't good," I said in a pseudo-knowledgeable manner. (Not rocket science I might add).

"That sounds like I'm bribing him!" was the instantaneous reply.

"No, it's called behavior modification," was the clever rejoinder.

A litany of questions tumbled out: "What about not taking the time-outs at home? The hitting? Saying mean things?! Grandparents going to the Ozarks?!"

"Those come in time…we have to focus on one thing at a time. If you try too many things at once nothing will work. Inconsistency is magnified. You keep a log of the program and we modify it if necessary. You'll win this one!" I said, covertly crossing my fingers behind my back.

"I'll try," was the reply. Over the years, I've learned that 'I'll try' is akin to "I'll say I'll do it to shut you up, but it has a snowball's chance in hell of actually succeeding and I'll try it for 30 seconds."

"Let's meet next Thursday to see how the program went—just remember, it often gets worse before it gets better!"

"Worse?!?!?! Arrrggghhhhh!!!" was the wide-eyed reply, delivered through clenched teeth.

Besides what can go wrong? Well there are numerous possibilities: 1) Hudson deems the contents of the grab bag to be crummy and not worth a hoot; 2) Hudson gets kicked out of preschool number 6, thereby effectively terminating the program before it even gets going; 3) He secretly hides the Bionicals so they can't be taken away; 4) Hudson ups the ante, making mom, the teacher, the principal, the custodian, and anyone else with whom he comes in contact, more miserable and likely to surrender; 5) Hudson develops a fondness for the Red Chair; 6) He develops a greater fondness for trips to the principal; or 7) His grandparents stay in the Ozarks for ever and ever.

I opened the door and Mom strutted out in a seemingly confident, determined manner, ready to take on the hellion of the Red Chair, Hudson.

Just as I was closing the door I heard Hudson pipe up:

"I'm not wearing my stupid seatbelt in the stupid van! I want a Happy Meal for dinner! Now! Or I'll chop your head off!"

No response from Mom, except for a wimpy, "We'll see."

I gently, but quickly closed the door, not hearing any more of the rather one-sided conversation that was unfolding. Diagnosis? Oppositional defiant disorder, ADHD maybe, poor parenting? Man of the house syndrome? As I was writing some notes, when out of the blue, another theme about discipline popped into my head! The unwavering discipline, the steeled code of conduct, the oath to totally disregard one's own well being in order to protect others…yes, that's right—the legendary, the elite— THE LINCOLN SCHOOL SAFETY PATROL!!!

CHAPTER 12
The School Safety Patrol (and Band)

From 6th through 9th grade the epitome of cool was to be a bona fide member of the school safety patrol! It was the ultimate badge of honor to wear the yellow belt of distinction that circled your hips, had a strap come up from the right back hip, looped over your left shoulder and clipped over your front right hip. Without doubt, it was very stylish and complex attire. The essence of the safety patroller's important assignment was to stand on a desolate street corner, in all types of weather, at various distances from the school, and help the younger kids cross the street. They had to be pretty young—otherwise they wouldn't listen to you. In the case of older kids you simply authoritatively walked across the street with them, trying to stay a step or two ahead so at least it looked like you were in control. Sometimes, in order to do so, you had to take really fast, giant steps—almost looked like the Nazi SS goose-stepping in a parade (we used to see that a lot on TV). Richard Bowdamon was particularly crafty in that regard. He would typically saunter up to the corner and then blast off like a banshee, causing the hapless, unsuspecting safety-patroller to madly dash in an often futile effort to get in front of him. Then Richard, chuckling with glee, would stop suddenly, sometimes unbeknownst to barreling-forward safety patroller who by then looked like he was doing the funky chicken in the middle of the street. On certain days Richard found the resolve to do this to up to 10 patrollers in a row, taking a circuitous route to school while keeping himself highly amused. He was the bane of the safety patrollers, particularly the 6th and 7th graders!

I'm not sure how one actually got to be on the patrol, but I think it had something to do with good grades or maybe based on a preliminary scouting report of power walking potential observed in gym class that was provided by Mr. Bentz, the gym teacher. Georgie the Cop (aka Sgt. Mueller to his face) was the main crossing guy (who directed everyone who crossed Anderson Avenue right in front of the school). He was in charge of the safety patrol and if you were lucky enough to be selected, he sent a personalized letter saying that you were *recommended*! The letter was pretty official looking, coming from the Fairview Police Department and all. Upon receipt, Pop took great delight in repeatedly asking Philip and me which one of us did something to warrant a disciplinary letter from the police. This usually elicited wailing, tears, and a confession of some heretofore secret transgression that typically was unrelated to anything. When Philip received his letter and was subject to the subterfuge, he confessed to looking up one of the Limbardo twin's dresses in the old 'drop the pencil' ruse, earning him a swat to the back of the head. Come to think of it, the invitation probably was based on grades and student deportment (another word we didn't know)—effectively and immediately eliminating Dougie and Paulie. It was too bad that Dougie wasn't eligible—he would have put a stop to Richard's antics simply by tripping him, clothes-lining him, or using the spiffy yellow belt-thing as a lasso! As a last resort he might have simply punched him in the head.

Georgie took his job very seriously. Patrollers were mandated to be at their post 30 minutes before the bell rang—unfortunately most patrollers were late, causing Georgie much anguish. I always suspected that they were using those cookoo clocks from Hoboken as their main timepiece and that those things ran slowly. Georgie was rumored to mutter barely audible threats of disenfranchisement on a daily basis to the laggard patrollers. Georgie was also noted to handle his whistle with impeccable precision, and could freeze a second grader in midstep with a piercing blast and a stern raising of his white-gloved hand, if they so much as began to think of venturing off the curb before he gave his okay.

"Glint—I heard you were late again today!"

"Sorry Sgt. Mueller." 'How the heck did he know that when I was 10 blocks away?!?! Friggin' amazing! Unless of course there was a —SNITCH! (aka some patroller who wanted to quickly rise up through the ranks and get one of the plum corners with mostly little kids who listened!). Or could it possibly be Richard Bowdamon?'

Eddie Pressioto was assigned to McKinley Street, while my post was Henry Street (across from the Greek Church). Eddie took his safety patrolling very seriously –almost as much as Georgie the Cop. He made Georgie proud on numerous occasions. His punctuality was impeccable—hell he was typically 20-minutes early! In fact, it was rumored that Georgie had dropped Eddie's name to the Police Chief Brusci as someone to keep an eye on and groom for the future (because most people never moved more than 2 miles from Fairview, this was a reasonable course of action).

In his zealous enthusiasm for the patrol, Eddie sometime got carried away and actually tried to stop cars in his quest to make crossing safe for our young charges. Pop almost took him out on several occasions with the Batmobile, this after having completed a midnight shift and a few brewskies afterward, consumed allegedly to help him sleep better. On at least one occasion he had to screech to a stop mere inches away from Eddie (whose eyes got really, really big and whose whistle fell from his mouth limply). Pop was typically audible up to 3 blocks away after such an incident and he said bad things about Eddie's intelligence. Pop used English, not Italian. We all had whistles, but most of us didn't use them because the little ball didn't flutter like it was supposed to and patrollers were known to get lightheaded from the excessive effort—the resulting, wheezy 'tweet tweet-chirp chirp' sounded like a cross between a dying chicken and a cat in heat (we still didn't know what that actually meant except that the cat acted pretty damn weird!) To make matters worse, the god-awful sound was so distorted and wimpy it flat out was comical—further vitiating the already tenuous façade of our authority!

There was a finely honed system in place where Georgie would pass a 'come-on-in' message to the closest patrollers, who then, in turn, dutifully yelled to the next farthest one. This time-honored tradition continued down the line until the most distant kid would get the message and come in–followed by the next furthest, and so on. Unfortunately it didn't always work and on more than one occasion a poor patroller was marooned blocks away, guarding her post; alone, frozen, and desperately longing to be given the elusive signal. Once Filomena didn't get to school until almost lunch time—she said she finally became suspicious when no one needed to cross the street for two hours, this further complicated by a funeral procession of a zillion cars that started at the Greek Church, effectively blocking her view of the next corner for quite some time.

On one occasion, Mr. Rinaldi was driving his gleaming black Studebaker down McKinley Street—the car was virtually spotless because he washed it every weekend, this followed by a waxing, applied with loving care. He hummed Italian songs as he waxed (and sometimes belted out the words like he was in an opera—unfortunately, we didn't exactly know what an opera was but we overheard Mrs. Clerico say that). Dougie said there were numerous cuss words embedded in the tunes as Mr. Rinaldi merrily hummed away, once again, saying this in a very convincing manner. We were able to decipher Mr. Rinaldi's favorite tune—something like:

"Whenna' da' moon hita your eye lika' bigga pizza pie—that's amoron!" (at least we *did* know what a moron was thanks to the Three Stooges!)

On that fateful day he was on his way to the deli when Larry (a little chubby 1st grader) stepped off the McKinley Street curb right into the path of the speeding, black chariot! Ye gads! Danger staring Eddie, the safety patrol icon, right square in the eyes! A tragedy unfolding right in front of him! Without flinching, with reckless abandon and cat-like agility (sort of), he immediately sprung into action!

"Tweet! Chirp! Gaack! Wheeze!"— a cacophony of strange sounds emanating at a whopping 27 decibels from that whistle tightly clenched between Eddie's teeth. Eddie was turning quite red in the face from the extraordinary effort but, nonetheless, he launched almost to the middle of the street, and smartly snapped his right hand in an authoritative, crisp "stop" signal that he was convinced could freeze a stampeding herd of elephants in their tracks.

"Whatta' the hell is that screwy kida' doing witta' stupid yellow belt and dema' white gloves!?!?" Mr. Rinaldi incredulously screamed to himself. (Yes, Eddie even had white gloves, emulating Georgie the Cop. Eddie said it made it easier to see his hands—I thought it made him look like Clarabell). In this case, when it became obvious that one raised

white-gloved hand didn't work, Eddie then raised both hands simultaneously in an effort to double the effectiveness of his authoritative gesture.
Unfortunately, he simply looked like some guy surrendering in a John
Wayne movie or perhaps Frankenstein chasing the villagers outside the
castle.

"Now whatta' dat nut job doing? Ah fungool! Get da' hella outta' da'
way kid!!" he bellowed out of the driver's side window (it was always
open no matter what the weather to let out the smoke from the ubiquitous, infamous 'guinea rolls'), "You' gonna getta killed!"

HONK, HONK, HONK! Blared Mr. Rinaldi's very loud Studebaker
horn as the highly polished nose of the hood lined up in a direct trajec-
tory toward Eddie's sternum.

"Getta' the hell outta' da' way you shitaful brains—I tella' you fadda'!"
(probably at Fritz's tavern).

By that time Larry had wheeled around and bolted back to the corner from which he came, leaving noble Eddie to deal with the wrath of
the Studebaker totally on his own. Seeing this, Eddie bolted to the other
corner while Mr. Rinaldi hung a wicked right turn, all the while glaring
out his window and saying many things in Italian that we had not heard
before. The amazing thing was how he wildly waved both of his hands
yet kept the Studebaker on course, seemingly turning on a dime! His
voice faded in the distance.

Eddie was holding on to the street sign, his whistle still in his mouth,
his red and white knit hat flattened in the middle of the street—now
decorated with tire tracks. It had some type of snowflake pattern (even
though it wasn't Christmas). I personally thought it looked better with
the muted black tire-track overlay. He slowly looked both ways and
gingerly picked up his hat and put it back on, finally spitting out his mal-
functioning whistle. Eddie was pretty pale and it sort of matched his hat.

Larry never even thanked Eddie for saving his life that fateful day. By the time Georgie the Cop heard about the remarkable feat of heroism, the tale had expanded in scope considerably, including that it was a blind kid with polio who was searching for his lost seeing-eye dog who only had 3 legs but who had saved a platoon of soldiers in the war! Eddie had single-handedly stopped a careening semi truck whose brakes had failed. Nonetheless he put Eddie up for a commendation—a sure way to get to the highly coveted Safety Patrol Hall of Fame and paving the way for a future job with the elite Fairview police!

However, by far the best thing about the safety patrol was the MARCHING BAND! Our first year (7th grade for the band) was the unveiling of the new, powder blue, satin-esque uniforms with matching boy-scout type powder blue hats and gold tassels. Big kids played the drums, girls played the bells (a walking xylophone-type contraption) while the rest of the kids played bugles of various sizes and stages of dis-repair—some were alleged to have survived the charge up San Juan Hill. Dougie reportedly overhead that the town fathers spent all the money on the uniforms, reportedly leaving $29.95 for instruments. There was also an honor guard and flag wavers. The buglers were all given Brasso in an attempt to make those horns gleam radiantly in the sunlight ($29.95 buys a lot of Brasso!). Unfortunately this approach was minimally suc-cessful. One of the best things about the bugles was the spit valve, which, when pressed would release a veritable tidal wave of spittle. This made many band members vie for the record of largest puddle—this somehow equating to some measure of manhood—an early example of "mine's bigger than yours!"

The Safety Patrol Band played at the 4th of July parade, the Memorial Day Parade, the Labor Day parade, the Little League parade, the Halloween parade (that always originated at the Orange and Black bus terminal), the Italian Day parade and any other incidental parade. Fairview had the most parades per capita than anyplace in New Jersey—and maybe even New York! Because of its size, the parades typically were fairly short. Unfortunately the band had a repertoire of approximately FIVE songs that were played in various sequences, depending on the secret code flashed by the drum major (none other than the brave, Eddie Pressioto!). Each song cleverly corresponded to the number of fingers raised on Eddie's gloved right hand (come to think of it that may have had something to do with the quota of five tunes!). Everyone wanted Eddie to flash the full five fingers—the secret code for the all time favorite—the primo song—the one that truly defined the band—"Moon Over Miami!"

We strutted smartly down the street in unison, anxiously anticipating Eddie's next mystery selection—except for Lenny Stueblood who had some type of tic (we called it a twitch in those days) that became very apparent whenever he clashed the cymbals and he would stick his tongue out the side of his mouth. He tended to seem a bit disoriented after a good clashing and occasionally wandered off into the spectators who ducked wildly lest they have an appendage (or worse yet, a head) wind up sandwiched between the two gleaming, deadly saucers of metal! He typically was redirected back into the line by strategically placed shoves and stiff arms. The frequency of these forays into the onlookers was directly related to Lenny working himself into a clashing frenzy during renditions of Moon Over Miami, where cymbal dexterity is a critical component. More #5's, more forays, this tending to damper the enthusiasm of other band members. Lenny became overzealous on occasion and added extra clashes that actually went with the music approximately 25% of the time. In an attempt at containment, we sandwiched him between William and Gerald, two rather large, portly baritone horn guys who could: a) hide him from the spectators, and, b) hip check him back into line if the need arose. This was moderately effective.

There was the occasional dropping of the mallet by one of the bell girls (Lena Linzetti was a frequent dropper) which then caused a domino effect. This was particularly problematic in the Little League parade where the teams lined up in rows, marching forward but looking sideways and waving to their relatives (who comprised 98% of the bystanders) applauding at the curbs. Once, half the Cigolini and Coop teams went down sprawling in the street during such a maneuver, raising heckles from onlookers.

"Whatsa' da madda' witha you kids—you drinka' da booze? Ha! Ha! Ha!" bellowed Mr. Rinaldi who was quite delighted at his own sharp wit and the instantaneous spontaneity of his humor. Mr. Stannoni thought it was quite funny as well, but the purple on his teeth suggested he had been hitting the grappa again and may have been biased.

By far the crown jewel of being a member of the Safety Patrol Band was the trip to Washington D.C. for the annual drum and bugle corps competition. This trip would include deluxe accommodations at a prestigious 2-star hotel (which was okay because nobody from Fairview ever stayed at a hotel –the only one in Fairview (that was even seedy by Fairview standards) had long closed and was replaced by the bank with an actual drive-through window). There would also be trips to historical sites such as the Capitol, various monuments, Mt. Vernon, Arlington Cemetery, and places to eat (nothing like the Horn and Hardart Automats that we went to feast at in New York, though). If the band did well in the competition someone would call ahead so that when the busses pulled back into town on Sunday night the streets would be lined with proud populace of Fairview (aka relatives of the band members and their pets). Apparently this happened once or twice in the long history of this proud contingent. We would never know what the outcome of the competition was until we were told the secret at the outskirts of the borough—this led to a level of anxious anticipation that was almost unbearable! Band members were elated even if we placed 20th (I think there might have been 22 bands in the competition).

This was also where we learned the concept of "the moon" from upper classmen. We were highly suggestible at that age and it looked like great fun; but when Ricky Boatman, a 7th grader, was nabbed in the act (also called pressing the ham) by the principal, Mr. Phillips, the attraction waned. It wasn't pretty to begin with, but the verbal harangue that rained down on hapless Ricky was monumental—plus he was moved to the seat behind the bus driver, right next to Mr. Phillips, and was mandated to sit on his hands and stare straight ahead for the rest of the trip.

Also during the trip, when at the hotel, the young adolescents began to engage in pranks (water guns, water balloons, de-pantsing, locking depantsed roommates out in the hall) and in premiering their various stages of secondary development (flashing, running around in jockey shorts, displaying new-found areas of body hair). Sonja Hoftess, a 9th grader, was one such exhibitionist who had advanced stages of orb development and was rumored to lift her top to display these assets to tourists, doormen, and members of other bands in adjoining hotels. We often tried to find out what room she was in just in case our window might offer the possibility of a gander. Based on these hotel adventures, many male band members were given clever, descriptive nicknames that would follow them for months: "hairless," "peanuts," "boner boy," "humongo" and others not fit to repeat.

For many band members, this was their first foray out of Fairview. This issue was potentially problematic when drinking water with new microbes—causing a domestic version of Montezuma's Revenge (despite microbial resistance developed in response to the Palisades Amusement Park pool flora)! I recall one trip to Mt. Vernon where the call of nature kept yodeling to the point that several of us first-timers who, before we literally exploded, had to periodically dash down off the trail into the gullies below, while others stood guard on the trail and pointed away to mysterious things in the trees, causing tourists to divert their gaze from the agonizing business that was transpiring down there. Only the moans, flatulence, and anguished grunts occasionally gave us away. Luckily this malady had settled down by the day of the competition!

The alternating sightseeing/hotel exploits schedule went on for several days, whereupon it was time for the big event! We woke up early, got dressed in our fine garb and were ready to go in no time! The anxious patrollers piled off the busses in the staging area and immediately noticed that other bands with equally spiffy uniforms and much shinier horns were warming up as well. There was a cacophony of sounds, the timbre simply awe-inspiring (although some seemed to be off-key). Lenny's cymbal clashing was particularly notable—I didn't realize that cymbal-players needed to tune up!

When our number was called, we lined up and wheeled smartly to the left—except for Lenny who somehow evaded Gerald and William and turned less smartly to the right, careening into unsuspecting members of an adjacent band, clashing the cymbals with unbridled passion in the process. This was resolved, and after several renditions of our 5-song repertoire in our trek down the avenue (Eddie was nervous and kept raising the same number of fingers several times in a row), we were within sight of —THE REVIEWING STAND! We marched in place, the drummers keeping time ("boom boom boom, dada boom, boom, boom). Then it was time and Eddie raised his hand—FIVE FINGERS!!! Moon Over Miami!!!! Yeehah! We were off— flags waving, and drums, and bells, and horns and cymbals, all working in fine-tuned harmony (mostly). When we arrived at the stand, our coveted, premier tune flowing melodiously, we snapped our heads to the left as we marched forward—luckily without any major incidents. Someone even said the President of the United States was there! However the veracity of the reporter, Sonja, was questionable, particularly since she said she saw him looking at her boobs. Then, seemingly in a flash, it was over. Back to the hotel, pack up the stuff and load up the busses—each safety patroller secretly wondering did we win the big kahuna!?!? First! Eighth! Third! Twentieth! (no one wanted that one overtly). On the return journey, the drone of the bus lulled many of us to sleep, anticipatory smiles on our cherubic faces—like the night before Christmas. We eventually made it back to Fairview. Suddenly, horns blared!!—jolting many band members from their happy sleep! We won something!! What!?! Who cares-it's SOMETHING!!! The bus erupted with unbridled glee and maniacal cheering and bouncing (except for Ricky the reformed mooner who had to yell while still sitting on his hands and facing forward). There was Mrs. Winn, walking Fluffy (actually more like dragging Fluffy who for all appearances looked dead)! She was waving wildly! And Paulie! And Dougie!! Little Al!! Charlie!! Hooray! As it turns out we got 9th place which we agreed was pretty good—heck it was at least in the top half!

Good old reliable #5—Moon Over Miami!

CHAPTER 13
Session with the Electronic Kid

Today's calendar included Allan Whatsky, aka Mr. Electronica. Before every appointment he sat in the waiting room totally mesmerized by his iPod touchamatic (or something like that)—it contained games, movies, songs, photos, maps, weather reports, horoscopes, recipes and direct, wireless connection to the international space station. Allan had ear buds on but the volume was such that the sounds (allegedly music) could be heard through the closed door. This raised questions regarding Allan's hammer-anvil-stirrup connections. Allan's mother, Esther was a short woman with fluffy reddish-hued hair, red rouged cheeks and lipstick and a voice that sounded like George Costanza's mother on Seinfeld re-runs (but even more whiny and grating). Esther was a single mom, having divorced Allan's dad some 10 years earlier—"that cheap bum never paid me a dime!" was her mantra.

Allan was a squat, chubby, 12-year old with short blond hair, thick round glasses (giving him a Harry Potter look) and a penchant for wearing clothes combinations that he undoubtedly selected in the dark.

Apparently the only prerequisite for clothing selection was that there had to be many pockets, these for the iPod, iphone, extra earbuds, DS, iPod connector for the car, extra games, snacks, gum, hamster, and other assorted items. At one point a while back he had a pager, but that became too passé.

His phone typically was on vibrate mode for clandestine alerting and Allan had it configured to monitor a vast array of sites: Hotmail, AOL, Facebook, MySpace, Twitter, Pinterest, YouTube, NASA, NYSE, and text messages, just to name a few. Monitoring these sites was a 24/7 job and Allan was definitely up for it! He was an electronicsmeister par excellence! Allan was very adept at switching from his phone to his iPod and back again instantly and in a seamless fashion. He could also make it a trifecta with the addition of an iPad. Hell he could have a different person (and face) on each. Allan was phenomenally fast when typing with his two thumbs on the minute keyboard—his, without doubt, were the fastest thumbs around.

I, too, have a keyboard on my Blackberry (which Allan referred to as an antique). However I believe that due to evolution and the resultant Darwinian natural selection, I am no match for the thumb dexterity and fine-motor coordination of the Gen-Xers or Millenials. Essentially, I (and many of my contemporaries) am a texting Neanderthal! Plus, I have no understanding of the new language that has evolved: OMG, BVD, K, LOL, LMAO, TTYL, RIP, OK (that one I know), SOB (that one too), etc. ('etc' is never used by true texters). Give me Latin any day! Terra, terrae, terram, terrae—now that's something decodable!

JRKjo, QGAtk-PV.—My first attempt at 'Hello, what's up?', the result of confusion with the 'alt', arrow up, delete, and shift keys, in addition to repeatedly hitting several at the same time because of maladroit, fat thumb syndrome. Anyway, I prefer to simply talk on the phone, as this was the original purpose of the device.

"So Allan, your Mom said you've been spending a lot of time on Facebook," I said in my opener.

"You bet doc! Just found out Ralphie is at the pet store to get another parakeet because the one he had croaked."

"He put that on Facebook?"

"Yeah, and he said the old bird was SOL!"

"SOL"?

"Damn right! FOD!!"

"FOD??" (seems like I was asking all the questions by this point).

"Yup" he replied (I did not pursue further clarification of these apparently run-of-the-mill acronyms, opting for the façade that I knew what was going on).

I had the distinct feeling that I was at a marked disadvantage in this dialogue and that things were not going to improve in the foreseeable future. I realized there could be a fortune to be made in a "Texting Acronyms for Older Dummies" book. Perhaps I could discuss this project with Allan and enlist his expertise as a co-author. On second thought, probably not, as that may get awfully close to some ethical issues, I suspect.

"Ralphie also said his rash was worse and that he was going to see Dr. Wienman."

"Why would he post that?" I queried.

"So that everyone would know!" he replied almost indignantly (My clinical skills enabled me to detect that Allan perhaps was thinking that I had the logical sense of Bozo). So much for maintaining any sense of anonymity in the world.

"He even took a picture of his dead parakeet and put it on his Facebook page."

'Wonderful,' I thought to myself.

"It looked like it was sleeping, laying on its back and all. Feet were sticking straight up, though. Actually, I don't think birds sleep on their backs."

"Allan, you're speaking really loudly—mind taking the earphones off?" I asked.

"Doc they're earbuds" he replied pedantically as his pants pocket hummed. "Just a second Dr. Wayward," Allan blurted, as he retrieved his phone and rapidly read a message and responded in 12 nanoseconds. He was back with me in a flash—"you were saying?"

"How about we invite Mom in now?"

"Sure!" Allan said as his pocket hummed once again. This time he dispatched his response in a mere 9 nanoseconds!

Allan's Mom came in for some family work and immediately launched into her laundry list of complaints (many of which were relatively valid).

"He's always with the iPhone or iPod or iPad or something with an 'I'—bedtime, bathroom, at the table, in school, on his skateboard, on his bike, in the car, in the bathtub!" she wailed. "I can't talk to him because he's always fiddling with one of those damn electronic things!!"

"Not all the time!" Allan retorted, though somewhat unconvincingly.

"He even does the phone thing when he's on his computer—or his iPod or even his DS!" she whined.

"Hey mom, I can multitask!" was his reply.

"If only he could do as well at school!" she lamented in a very Jewish-grandmotherly exasperated way (Italian grandmothers had similar lamenting skills).

I recalled driving past school busses in the morning, gazing in on legions of kids with wires dangling from their ears and looking downward in unison, the object of their gaze obscured by the window line (the object probably being a phone or an iPod). Not one was looking sideways to the traveling companion in the adjacent seat or even out the window—all were enveloped in a cocoon of total psychological isolation! Ye gads!

I see it coming—We will simply not talk to each other anymore! Vocal cords will simply wither away. Even if the person is right next to you, proper etiquette will be to text (NOT talk), using a new type of shorthand unbeknownst to the human race a mere 5 years ago! I have witnessed this already occurring on the school busses! Is this evolution or are we doomed!? Wow, that was some pretty deep existential thinking from ol' Doc Wayward even if I do say so myself!

I see it happening in the fitness clubs across America! Everyone wired up, oblivious to the gargling screams from the guy turning blue because he is being crushed by the barbell during a bench press gone awry! Dr. Ice Tea Rappa', rapping happily and loudly away—the listener totally oblivious to the sounds of the outside world.

"Boopada, boopada, F**k you motha'f***er!" from the earbuds.

"Gaak! Gaak!" from the bluish-colored bench presser.

It already happens in car rides! No counting cars or looking for letters on license plates on family trips. Instead, don't talk—just watch the DVD in one of the six players strategically located in each minivan, even on a 1/10th mile drive to the local Walgreens! The only conversation might involve DVD selection or complaints about volume!

Photos of everything taken by phones, or tablets, or iPods,—blackmail opportunities galore! (Actually, that might have made the band trips even more interesting back then! Particularly with Sonja).

Everyone knows where everyone is at any given moment! Everywhere! GPS is status quo. Need directions to Hoboken? No problem now!

"Dr. Wayward—are you listening?"

"Whoops—reality check!"

"Allan's grades are terrible—I had to lock up the Wii and X-box!! Then I had to take the computer away so he couldn't Skype anyone during homework time!"

"I use Google and Wikipedia to answer my homework questions!" Allan said emphatically,

"I need access!"

"I caught you at 2 a.m. texting while you were under the sheets! And you wouldn't say who it was! There must be millions of kids going without sleep!"

"Hey Dr. Wayward—I saw satellite pictures of your house on Google!" Allan said, adroitly changing the course of the conversation.

"You did?" I asked incredulously, falling for the adroit change in course.

"Yeah, and I also saw you wrote a couple of books and stuff," he continued.

"You did?" I replied, falling for the ruse even further. By this point I totally forgot about the midnight textarama and was soaking up the praise.

'So much for anonymity even if you really wanted anonymity—even without Facebook!' I mused.

In a weak effort to tie something more important and tangible into the grade issue I asked, "Any ideas about what you would like to do when you get older?"

"Videogame developer," was the immediate reply.

"Imagine that!" I blurted out before the frontal lobes had inhibited the urge. That effectively deflated any further attempt to underscore long-term ramifications of electronically screwing around.

"Maybe I'll develop a Windows 12! Or a new social media site—or some homework apps!"

More ring-around-the-rosy arguments followed without much resolution. I began to reminisce about cutting-edge electronics unveiled during my own childhood—major innovations that now seem to pale in comparison to the complexities of cellphones, laptops, iPads, solar lights, videogames, weedwackers, clap-sensitive light switches and Al Gore's internet....give me a transistor radio any day!

CHAPTER 14
Historic Electronic Milestones in the Old Days

Five or more decades ago, a colossal event happened at the border of Fairview and North Bergen. All the towns ran together back then and signs were at a premium. What was perplexing for those of us who would think about things more complicated than when the Good Humor ice cream truck would be coming by, was the fact that North Bergen was in Hudson County and Fairview was in Bergen County. This raised the issue of why Fairview wasn't called South Bergen or why North Bergen wasn't called North Hudson. This oddity never seemed to bother Paulie or Dougie, but I suspected the founding fathers of each town were confused or maybe didn't have maps. Anyhow, the colossal event was—the gala, fantastic, grand opening of FOOD FAIR!!! One of the first of the new breed of stores—the supermarket! While this affair afforded the opportunity to sample the latest in tasty, culinary delights, a much more important highlight was the debut of the electronic marvel, *the automatic opening doors!* It was the talk of the town for months!

This device of the future was amazing to those of us who were already easily amazed—particularly Dougie and Paulie. All you had to do was step on a rubber mat in front of the door and, viola, the doors would swing wide open! Just like that! You could strut right in like a real big shot. The same set-up was on the inside, allowing Food Fair customers to pull their overflowing, two-wheeled cart right out the portal and clatter and squeak down the block without having to touch the door! Paulie didn't quite get the inside-out thing—frequently getting stuck between the opening door and the protective metal rail. In fact, Philip took great delight in hiding behind the pyramid of Coco Marsh jars and stealthly tapping his foot on the runner whenever he spied Paulie meandering in front of the exit.

Meander, meander.

Quick step.

Thump! "Arrgghhhh!"

It was great sport and occasionally an unsuspecting Lady in Black, who was semi-mesmerized while participating in a walking rosary mantra, became the victim. They also said things in Italian, but not with as much vigor or emphasis as did Mr. Rinaldi. (Their elocution often was made difficult by a lack of teeth). After they did so, they made numerous signs of the cross. Dougie also was an occasional victim—we could tell when he 'kissed the door' with his face because of the sudden, unbridled volley of F-words, peppered with select phrases he had learned by carefully observing Mr. Rinaldi and Mr. Stannoni when they were in a particularly animated state. Again to the discerning ear, many sounded like F-words with an accent, staccato timing, and more long vowels. These displays typically were not followed by a sign of the cross.

These doors were simply baffling! A true mind-boggling mystery! A step farther into the future than even Sputnik! Dougie said they ran by radar and most of us believed him. I didn't recall that you had to step on something to make radar work, but Dougie's argument was very persuasive, made more so by liberal description of x-rays thrown in for emphasis. Ritchie Freganosi said that his dad told him the secret mechanism involved a heat sensor. In this case, I (Glint, the Doubting Thomas), wondered how your foot gave off enough heat to go through your Keds sneaker (or even a Thom McCann Snap-jack!). Paulie's hypothesis was more simplistic (not surprising)—he thought someone was hidden inside the store with a periscope and the person pressed a button whenever anyone came close to the doors. I pragmatically wondered what happened when the button presser left the button unattended like if he had to really go to the bathroom—this explanation also made me skeptical. Not to mention that Paulie simply was not nearly as persuasive as Dougie! It was obvious that the seeds of scientific inquiry were already sprouting in the mind of young Glint.

Eddie had the record for consecutively going in and out of Food Fair's magical doors—a whopping 43 times! Ritchie was on the verge of breaking that Guiness-worthy number, but was chased away by this really big grocery bagger kid that the manager (who always wore a short-sleeved white shirt and bowtie) dispatched in pursuit of the unsuspecting Ritchie, after having seen him go in and out of the doors numerous times. Ritchie added a few more in-and-outs with the bagger kid in hot pursuit, but then the brute simply waited outside while Ritchie did his 42nd lap. That bagger kid was friggin' strong! We were amazed how far Ritchie flew through the air after a seemingly effortless toss, preceded by a one-handed snatch of Ritchie's coat collar. I happened to be inside by the Bosco display (another chocolate syrup that was in direct competition with Coco Marsh) and saw Ritchie sort of flapping his arms as he sailed past the spiffy, brand new Food Fair windows. He looked like he was flying, at least for a second or two before he disappeared. Several Ladies in Black who witnessed this gravity-defying spectacle were noted to make signs of the cross.

Actually, what was more interesting was this guy named Patsy who, at the same time as Ritchie was flying, just so happened to be washing his face in the large, pickle barrel—he also bit a few and threw them back in. To my yet-untrained eye, I had previously surmised that Patsy seemed a bit unusual, and when I mentioned this, Pop said it was due to the war. I had little knowledge of diagnostic nomenclature at the time but definitely thought Patsy was a few sandwiches short of a picnic (I heard Philip say that once). Mom would do a sign of the cross whenever she saw old Patsy shuffle by. He was a rather disheveled fellow, and he made Dougie's wardrobe look like it was a fashion statement, recently arrived from Macy's! It was actually difficult to tell the color of his clothes—stain atop stain gave his ample pants a paisley patina.

Patsy used to play piano for the volunteer fireman after their Friday night softball games. The firemen kept giving him beer and food (mostly beer by my informal observation) and Patsy would play the entire night. Many tunes sounded very similar to the discerning ear. Unfortunately, Patsy did not know Moon Over Miami. This disheveled maestro offered a running commentary while he played—unfortunately this involved him talking to and answering himself, exclusively. Sometimes it looked like he was talking to the beer glass. Occasionally he would belt out a few lines to accompany the piano music, but this usually happened toward the end of the night, and by that time Patsy was not easily understood. Not being a psychologist yet I also considered this behavior to be highly peculiar. Dougie said the Food Fair door radar fried Patsy's brain. This I knew was erroneous because Patsy was acting peculiar at the firehouse even before the Food Fair Grand Opening! (My analytical thinking at that tender, young age was a harbinger of things to come!) Occasionally Patsy was nowhere to be found and a stand-in, this skinny black guy named "Porkchop" provided entertainment. He sang more and played funky tunes that had the firemen dancing (mostly with each other because the wives were: a) embarrassed to dance with them, and b) had not drunk ample amounts of beer so as to loosen up their leg muscles). I recall that Porkchop mysteriously disappeared after a few guest appearances. Dougie said he was a pimp and that someone cut his throat. We didn't exactly know what a pimp was, nor were we aware of the consequences of getting one's throat cut although Eddie said he saw Johnnie the Barber accidentally do that when he was shaving Mr. Tavanno (again it was towards the end of the day after many trips to the back room).

Back to the automatic doors.

Paulie also tried to break Eddie's in-and-out-the-door record, but he kept losing count at around 27 or so. I think he might have gotten distracted by Mr. Rinaldi who sometimes considered himself the Food Fair vigilante.

"Twenty-three, twenty-four...."

"Hey you stupida' kid—why you keep going inna' and outta' da' door—you a dumma' bell or something?!?"

"Twenty...two?"

"You gonna; break data' speciala door! Then no more speciala' door for dis town! I'm gonna' tella da manager and he gonna' call da' cops— and no Coop baseball for you either!"

Twenty-one."

Meanwhile, the bagger boys and the guy with the bowtie were escorting Patsy out through those amazing doors. Patsy was very red and sweaty and he was yelling something about not even giving any of those f***ing pickles to his dog! I didn't even know Patsy had a dog! And one that ate pickles to boot! This further confused Paulie's count and gave Mr. Rinaldi yet another opportunity to unleash his droll and pithy comments. Our infatuation with Food Fair lasted for quite some time!

A new, *personal* electronic device that hit the scene by storm was the coveted, fantastic, TRANSISTOR RADIO!—invented in Japan way before 8 track tapes or cassettes! What a marvel! It fit right in your hand, had a little speaker (about the size of a quarter on the deluxe models), a 2-foot telescoping antenna (or somewhere close to that), it ran on a single battery, and you could plug in an earphone! (one ear only). It was the all-time epitome of coolness!

"Muddy river, blah, blah skritch."

"I'll never love blah, crackle, crackle." (sometimes even the almost 2-foot long antenna didn't work quite right in picking up one of the myriad [a total of 3] AM stations!)

Dougie didn't have one of these wonders. Paulie sold his brother's for $5.00—again, his brother wasn't happy with Paulie and mentioned that he strongly doubted they had the same parents and therefore were most likely not related.

Eddie had one with a premium, genuine leather carrying case, complete with a hand strap—unfortunately, it melted when he left it out in the sun. I didn't know that leather melted, but Eddie was pretty convinced it did, his opinion further substantiated by the sales clerk at Woolworth's who sold him the item. We made a dashing display, strutting down the sidewalk with radios held to our ears, occasionally making out words from the static. They had this call-in program where a song that received the most call in votes would be played every 20 minutes! We heard Fats Domino's "Blueberry Hill" at least 62 times on one Saturday. The only problem was that the radios made Fats sound like he was pinching his nose as he sang—sort of like one of the Chipmunks:

"I found my crackle, crackle thrill on Bluecrackle crill zzzttt Hill."
Luckily,we already knew the words.

This was a minor inconvenience, given the fact that we could hear
the music AND we were entirely mobile, this accomplished with only
one 9-volt battery!!! What could be more cool than that?!?! Heck we
even brought them to Little League games and Dodgeball—the number
of places you could bring your transistor radio was limitless! Dougie said
they were cheap because they were made in Japan—little did he know
that's exactly why we could buy them—they *were* cheap! Paulie was not
good at geography and swore that Japan was close to Switzerland or
Hoboken, the land where Mrs. Burton's cookoo-clock originated from.
Sometimes, in order to continue to be cool when the battery died, we
would still keep the earphone in and bob our heads from side to side.
Eddie was doing that one time until Paulie (of all people) noticed that
his earphone wasn't even plugged in! Eddie swore he was just trying to
loosen his neck.

Our interests gradually expanded over time to the next electronic
wonder—the spiffy, compact, Commodore reel-to-reel portable tape
recorder! Three-inch reels with delicate brown tape that you could use
over and over again (as long as the machine didn't eat it up and crinkle
it to the consistency of spaghetti!) Just slap the microphone up close
to a bigger radio (Emerson was a perennial favorite), press the record
and play buttons simultaneously, and you were in business! You could
even make like an announcer in between songs and, if you were really
good, you could fade out by carefully turning down the sound at the end.
For some reason, though, we never sounded like our idols, the WMCA
Good Guys!!

In our opinion, WMCA was by far the best radio station, beating
Cousin Brucie from WABC or even Murray the K! Be the first to call

in and win a yellow sweatshirt emblazoned with a smiley face and the bold 'WMCA Good Guy' logo (there was no WMCA Good Girl sweatshirt at that time). We listened daily to the DJ icons—Joe O'Brien, Harry Harrison, and of course, B. Mitchell Reed! Even more coveted was the 45 rpm record that you could win in the legendary 'name-it-and-claim-it' if you were the first to call in with the name of the song and artist!

"OK fans, lines are open!" B. Mitchell warbled.

A call to action! Damn rotary dial phone took forever (it was an antique even then!), so I used to dial all but the last number and hope that the time was right for the final '5' to rotate around before you were disconnected. There were many, many unfortunate false alarms! Plus when I pushed the limits of my speed dial frenzy, I often got Nasser Aftab's House of Carpets. I think many other fans did as well. Nasser's initial cheerfulness at the prospect of a rug sale quickly waned over the course of many an unprofitable evening. My household eventually advanced to push button status, further enhancing my call-in prowess.

B. Mitchell was our idol—we couldn't believe that an opportunity arose where we could see him— IN PERSON!!! Yessiree he said it loud and clear on the radio! He'd be there for the Sunday afternoon matinee at Palisades Amusement Park's world famous (everything there seemed to be world famous) outdoor amphitheater (fancy name for a rickety stage that backed up to the Palisades, with bench seats in front that were in dire need of paint). The stage actually was a few hundred feet from the pool lockers, right across from the flying cages. Luckily, I had gotten over my salt-water pool PTSD triggered by the near-drowning and the tomato-head escapades by then. I talked Ritchie and John Askaris into going. Anticipating crushing crowds, a mile long line (at least), and SRO at the 1 p.m. event, we arrived at the gates by 10 a.m. sharp so as to stake out prime seats for this once-in-a-lifetime opportunity!

"Whadda' ya' doin' here dis early on Sunday—don't you go to choi-ch??" queried the lady in the little booth at the Park entrance, "nuttin's open yet"! She looked like she was just rousing to the light of a new day, after having survived a busy Saturday night, probably having slept in the booth. It was difficult to understand her but this might have been influenced by her lack of teeth. Her toothlessness was accentuated by the brightest reddish orange lipstick that I had ever seen! It was like neon! Magnificent! We all stared at her lips for several very long minutes, our trance-like state interrupted by a strident:

"Hey!! I said it's fifty cents a head or get lost!" she said in a lispy fashion while squinting in the sunlight.

"We're here to see B. Mitchell Reed!!!! –and Randy and the Rainbows and some other really neat groups!!" John said pretty much hysterically. Actually, it was hysterically.

"Who the hell is dat?!? If you mean the band stand—dat doesn't start for 3 hours!"

Obviously she was simply ill informed and I wondered if she might be delirious after having perhaps actually slept in that little booth over-night. Or maybe she had already checked in hundreds of eager fans already and she was exhausted!

"We wanted to beat the crowds!" Ritchie piped up.

"What da' hell crowds are you tawkin' about?!?" she replied, her eye-brows raising upward like two brown caterpillars.

"B. Mitchell Reed has humongous crowds—quadrillions of fans lis-ten to him every night!" We knew she had to be pulling our collective legs!

"You kiddin' me?!?! Gimme da' 50 cents a head or get outta' heah!"

We gleefully forked over the coins and rushed down to the stage, right past the unmoving flying cages. Close by was the win-a-goldfish stand. That's where you threw ping-pong balls, trying to have one land in a microfishbowl that had approximately 1.5 mm of space between the lip and the entering ball. You had as much of a chance winning a goldfish as you did lightening striking the Freak Show with the two headed snake. If you did win a fish, it typically became a floater before you left the midway. Dougie said it was because the water in the bowl was colored (blue, green, red, etc.) and the ping pong ball gave the fish a concussion. Actually, they might have been dead to begin with—they were pretty far away. Luckily the stand hadn't opened yet—lest we would have been inadvertently sidetracked like moths to a flame.

Back to the preparations for the upcoming show.

Breathless, we staked out our seats in the very first row. Actually, that was relatively easy as we were the only living things in the entire amphitheater—maybe even in the entire park!

"This place is deserted—you sure it's today? John asked rather quizzically and perhaps a tad suspiciously.

"Sure it is! The gate lady knew about it didn't she?" I replied somewhat convincingly. "She was just playin' us for fools! We didn't fall for it!"

So we sat down in the front row and listened to our transistor radios—all tuned in WMCA—to see if there were any late-breaking announcements about B. Mitchell and the show. 10:10—it was going to be a long morning.

At about 12:30 this short, skinny black guy whose name was Lamont Jackson, said he was in the opening group, Sweet Soul something, and he would gladly give us his autograph. He wore a lot of rings and gold chains so we figured he was the real deal. His gold tooth sparkled in the sunlight. Besides, the name, Lamont Jackson, did sound a bit familiar. At least that's what Ritchie said.

By 12:35 there were 20 people (including us).

12:45—31 people (including us).

12:55—38 people, us included (John had this thing about counting things repeatedly back then).

1:05—B. Mitchell Reed strolls on stage and gazes out at the audience now consisting of a whopping 53 spectators (including some carnies sweeping up after last night). We screamed and yelled and jumped up and down—it took us several minutes before we realized we were the only members of the audience doing so. B. Mitchell looked at us somewhat quizzically.

"Ladies and gentlemen welcome to the WMCA World's Greatest Sunday Matinee—our first cool act—The Sweet Soul Sound!!"

Sure enough there was Lamont in white pants and a red sparkly shirt opened to his belly button. Those gold chains really stood out against his dark skin. He and his group were lip synching –sort of like Soul Train or maybe Hullabaloo. They were really loud.

"Hey there's our buddy Lamont—nice clothes—man he's cool!" Ritchie yelled.

There he was—hair pomped, slick footwork (a predecessor to the moon walk that we would hear about many decades later), sparkling all over in the sunlight, blowing kisses to the girl in the yellow dress that was quite revealing of her assets. Lamont looked like he might be the guy singing the high notes like Smokey Robinson but it was hard to tell because of the kiss blowing thing. Plus, sometimes his mouth was closed but the sounds still came through the speakers (and vice versa— Lamont had to work more on his delivery). A few more songs and it was B. Mitchell Reed again.

"Let's give these guys a round of applause!" The rest of the group had to pull Lamont off the stage as he was still blowing kisses to the girl with the assets.

"Yeehahh!!" I screamed.

"Cool cat!!" yelled John.

"I love you B, Mitchell and all the WMCA Good Guys forever and ever!" Ritchie screamed at the top of his lungs—reaching an amazing decibel level! I think Ritchie obviously became caught up in the moment.

A stunned silence descended upon the crowd. B. Mitchell had a frozen, rather cheesy smile plastered on his face. We did not turn around, but slowly sat down, staring straight ahead, sort of like the reformed mooner, Richard Bowdoin, did on the Safety Patrol bus. Ritchie obviously was a bit overzealous.

Luckily, out came Randy and the Rainbows. No band, just the Rainbows.

"Oh Denise scooby doo,"

Screams and applause.

"I'm in love with you Denise, scooby doo."

More screams and applause.

'Can't get much better than this!' I marveled. " It's soooo cool!" A few more songs and then things were coming to an end. Songs were shorter then—like 1 minute and 43 seconds—so groups either had a large repertoire or they sang the same songs multiple times.

"Hey! We need to get autographs!!" John bellowed after having an eureka moment. That's right! How could we forget?!?!

We couldn't rush the stage from the front because our heads just about peered over the edge even if we stood straight up. We saw Lamont go to the side of the stage earlier, so we traced his steps. Sure enough—stairs! We quickly ascended them, doing two at a time only to be stopped dead in our tracks by a burly off-duty cop with a large hotdog in his hand.

"Hey—where youse kids think you're goin'? Get outta' here! It's a restricted area!" (the last statement sounded pretty official to us).

"We want to get B Mitchell Reed's autograph!" screamed Ritchie.

"He's gone already kid!" was the burly reply.

"Shit""

"What?"

"Shoot!"

"Go home kid!"

As we dejectedly turned away, I gazed forlornly at Lamont's very stylish John Hancock—nice, but not good enough. Plus he spelled Glint wrong.

We caught the #22 bus for the ride home, listening absent mindedly to our transistor radios, futilely wishing that a name-it-and-claim-it would be in our future. Besides, B. Mitchell was coming on for his evening show.

"Turn dat crap off will ya?" a shrew-like woman squawked. We knew immediately that this denizen of the #22 bus wasn't a cool cat fan of the man—B. Mitchell! Alas! We were resigned to go home and watch the channel 9 Million Dollar Movie—back to back showings of Godzilla! And Mothra! And Rodan! A Japanese Cannes film fest! Sometimes on the weekends they played the same movie over and over, prompting us to vie for records like the most consecutive viewings of Mighty Joe Young. But that's another story.

Things were much more simple then.

CHAPTER 15
A Session with Daphne

Connie called, "Dr. Wayward, Miss Daphne and her mom are here."

"I'll be right there," I said, fumbling through my chart to see where we left off two weeks ago.

'Ah, yes, the intercepted text messages! Much anger, rebellion, denial, aiding and abetting!'

I met them at the door, "Hello ladies. Please come in and have a seat."

Daphne and her mother, Gail Forrester, were here for family work, and they bore a striking family resemblance. In fact, I was virtually certain that Gail had looked identical to her daughter when she, herself, was 16. Even now they looked like sisters: same height (about 5' 10"— with the platform shoes), blonde hair, sultry blue eyes with dark eyeliner, really thick lips with gloss, similar degree of tanning, thin bodies bordering on anorexia, short skirts, and similar assets, proudly jutting forward and only partially concealed by very tight, low cut tube tops. Sure as hell look like sisters! Except one was 40-something and the other, a mid-adolescent. The mid-adolescent looked twenty-something.

'Do they have the same plastic surgeon and botox guy? A family plan?' I wondered. Or maybe it's the hormones in chicken and milk that has been causing documented pubertal development at age 8. 'Don't keep looking at *them* like that,' I told myself. A very hard thing to not do, but made easier by the specter of malpractice!

"Last time we were discussing some problems with texting," I tossed out as an opening line.

"They call it sexting," Gail quickly replied in rather blunt clarification.

"Was not!! My clothes were on in those pictures!"

"But what was IN the photo? Go ahead and tell him—I DARE you!"

"My face wasn't even in it—I can't be identified!! Can't tell it was me! "

"Besides the fact that it came from *your* phone at 12 a.m., and those were *your* boobs—clothes on or no clothes on!"

'Oh boy, I thought—how do I intervene here? On second thought, do I really *want* to intervene? They seem to be doing just fine without me!'

"I heard muted clacking noises like someone was typing, went in her room and saw her on the bed with the phone in front of her chest! A camera noise and it was sent in a flash!"

"Can I ask who you were sext…er texting?" I finally asked.

"A friend."

"Tell Dr. Wayward how old your *friend* is!" Gail demanded. "No, I'll tell him—he's 22!!! And he's in college! And he's a bum!"

'Daphne can pass for that! No wonder!' I thought.

"Are you two dating?" I asked innocently.

"Not really—well sort of—sometimes. He's a good friend. I can talk to him about anything."

That clarified, I thought that there were some topics that probably came up repeatedly.

"He likes me for who I am and he understands me," Daphne continued between the snaps of her chewing gum.

This seemed more cerebral than I was willing to accept, given the Photoshop escapades. "So did you really send him a photo of your bo— er covered chest? If so, why?"

"To keep him interested—besides, lots of people do it, it sends a message that I really care about him," was the reply.

Sexting—A veritable boobathon! Chickens flying everywhere over the airways, the cell towers literally melting from the heat. What if aliens were evesdropping and had intercepted millions of pictures of covered and uncovered assets! All kinds of shapes and sizes! What about Victoria's Secret commercials? A bizarre comment on our culture—maybe even interpreted as a rather unusual greeting ritual. I wonder if aliens texted or sexted? Did they have assets?

"Dr. Wayward!" implored Daphne, bringing me back to the session, "whose side are you on?!?!"

'Whose side? NO side!! Therapy 101 books say no sides in family conflicts, no coalitions allowed in family work—particularly in the case of the Feuding Forresters!'

"No side!" I said with as much authority as I could muster. "We need to compromise and come to a mutually acceptable agreement (derived from Chapter 2 of Family Therapy 101)." This was said despite a likelihood ratio of 1 divided by infinity of it actually occurring.

"So Daphne will you stop doing that terrible behavior?" implored her Mom (doing so with a weird, wry smile).

'Hey, was that a wink too? An ENABLER!!—ye gads—I've cracked the puzzle! Damn, Wayward, you're good!'

"Only if I can still drive the car," she said coyly.

'A brand spanking new Mercedes E-350 4-matic' I might add.

"Okay," replied Gail without hesitation, "but…"

But Daphne was texting feverishly (but thankfully not taking any photos), thumbs in unison, accompanied by staccato gum snapping—almost as mesmerizing as the exploits of the Ladies In Black. A level of skill that would pose a challenge to the textmeister, Alan Watsky! What a text-off that would be!

"But Dad has to agree," Gail continued.

'Dad will vote in absentia,' I surmised. I saw dad one time when I first met the Forresters. He is a physician—surgeon I think, who was always on call, at a conference, performing a procedure, at a pharmaceutical rep event, winning the Nobel prize, or meeting with his broker. Come to think of it, maybe the phone thing is genetic—he kept stepping out of the room to take calls from his office. He even wore scrubs, including the footsie things that go over your shoes and a shower-cap like hat. Come to think of it, he looked pretty tan too. Maybe they have their own tanning bed in the basement! These last two sessions were going nowhere fast—what to do?!?! Have to resort to Chapter 22 of Therapy 101—Coming to Closure!

"So," I said, seizing the moment, "We have an agreement then?" (secretly crossing my fingers).

"Okay."

'Tap, tap, tap…tappetty tap tap—snap, snap snap" were the sounds emanating from Daphne's handheld and mouth, respectively.

"Just like that?" I asked incredulously, "So what are the specifics?"

"No more photos, but I can still see him sometimes, right?" piped up Daphne.

"Against my better judgment, but okay, precious," replied Mom.

'PRECIOUS? Very fitting,' I thought. "Shouldn't we have more specific details?"

"This should be sufficient," Gail quipped rather authoritatively, "I'm sure we can work out the rest of the minor points—besides I have a tennis lesson is 30 minutes."

'Why do I have an overwhelming tide of pessimism about this agreement actually working? If it was this easy, why wasn't it done before?' I give it 3 days before the program folds. No, maybe 2! Some much for closure!

"Actually I met this new guy, Jake at the basketball game—he's really cute and he's a Senior!" Daphne swooned.

I had forgotten about Daphne participating in approximately 90% of extracurricular activities available—cheerleading, volleyball, cross-country, tennis, Student Council, Key Club, Spanish Club, Habitat for Humanity, Peace Corps, 4-H, and soup kitchen volunteer.

Diagnosis? Cute girl, smart, loaded, popular, tanned. Probable augmentation Adolescent adjustment issues, clueless, enabling parents. As the late Piaget pegged it: she has a horizontal decalage—peaks and valleys with respect to psychological skills and levels of maturation. Not at the same level in each area for sure. High in physical maturity, social skills, and athletic ability; low in executive function and common sense.

This reminds me of my adolescent times and prurient interests—more specifically, the girls of Fairview!

CHAPTER 16
Phony Joanie

The neighborhood offered many opportunities to stoke the prurient interests of young male adolescents, whether it be tales of prowess from our older brethren, or evesdropped stories about a house named Lulu's on Anderson Avenue (I overheard, while secretly hiding in the cab of the fire engine at the firehouse after a Friday night softball game, that it was a *cat house*—odd thing was there were no cats there—not like Dougie's house). Paulie once tried to hide under the pool table to listen to fireman gossip more about Lulu's, but was quickly discovered when he yelled bloody murder after Patsy, who was scouting for more food and beer during a piano break, accidentally stepped on his hand. The house with the cats was reportedly was located about one block from the firehouse, according to our calculations.

Louie Ferrari was a self-proclaimed legend in terms of sexual prowess. A bacchanalian wonder! Paulie, Dougie, Ritchie, Eddie and I would sit on David Greenalches' stoop (most houses had stoops in Fairview) and marvel, wide-eyed at Louie's tales of conquest. He used many terms that were unknown to us, but they sounded really interesting: douche bag, scum bag, mother-f***er, come, jerk-off (accompanied by gestures that we all could easily imitate), whack off, the c-word, the p-word and many other words that one would not say in adult company. Not actually knowing the specifics of many verbs and other colorful descriptors, we nonetheless would nod and wryly smile whenever we heard one of the choice utterances, sometimes even mimicking the associated gesture. Although it was great fun, we constantly had to deal with the nagging fear that Louie or David might actually ask us what a given word meant!

"She had humongous boobs!" Louie chortled.

"She has big testicles and she knows it!" blurted Paulie proudly.

The dialogue stopped instantly and all eyes shifted to Paulie in a quizzical manner. Sensing imminent doom, Paulie quickly rejoined, "She likes big testicles and knows it and she has big tits!" Everyone shrugged and the discussion moved on. Paulie sometimes made his lack of mastery of stoop-learned words very apparent. We, on the other hand would furtively glance at Louie or David to gauge their reaction as we were responding, ever ready to reframe our statement at the slightest hint of a screw-up. I quickly learned that just laughing and nodding your head whenever anything was said by anyone was a pretty safe, all-purpose response—it covered funny, stupid, or totally confusing. Repeatedly spitting on the sidewalk also was a good distraction. The spit frequency was directly proportional to the level of excitement at the time. Occasionally touching one's own crotch as if rearranging assets was also deemed acceptable.

After listening to such mind-expanding discussion, we typically would stroll down the street, randomly spouting out new-found words to each other and laughing in unison each time one was unleashed. Spitting also was an associated activity. Dougie often threw f-words in between spits for added effect. Sometimes we even just used the first letters of the words, but this was sufficient and still produced the desired response.

"DB!!" followed by "whoohee, yeah, whoop whoop, you bet, ho, ho, ho!"

Many of the older Lincoln Street residents, upon witnessing this spectacle, would immediately stop what they were doing, clutch their brooms tightly (most residents had at least two or three) stare quizzically, and scrutinize our every move. Dougie, benefiting from past experience, was well trained to always stay out of broom range, just in case.

"Here coma' dose wisaguys again! Now what dida you do? sputtered Mr. Rinaldi, "You betta' not be doin' nutting !"

"Jerk off!!" spouted Dougie, trying out one of the new phrases of the day.

"Who callin' me a jerk?! I breaka' you ass! (again emphasizing the prevailing theme of inflicting some type of damage to someone's but-tocks—I never was quite sure how that would be accomplished, but it sounded ominous, nonetheless).

Then, like countless times before, coming around the corner from Fairview Avenue, there she was—Phony Joanie!!! Her name was coined because of the top-heaviness she displayed and which seemed to appear over the course of approximately 11 days! Dougie said this was the result of 'falsies', more specifically due to augmentation (too big of a word for Dougie) accomplished by ample use of FIBERFILL!!! Dougie said it was this foam stuff that you could buy at any well-stocked hardware store. Again, he was very persuasive in his argument. We were convinced, of course! Because of the preceding discussion and monologue by Louie, our collective interest in the appearance of Joanie was heightened. We were having, unbeknownst to us at the time, the first vestiges of an early adolescent testosterone storm!

In part because of this heightened interest, Ritchie and I came up with a clever idea for an *experiment* (another early indicator of a future in psychology!). What if we got Joanie's shirt wet?!?!— if there was fiberfill stuffed under there, it would soak up the water and Joanie's assets would droop down to her belly button at least! That would answer our question once and for all! The riddle of the rapid blooming solved! The plan bordered on unrivaled brilliance (perhaps a little south of the border, but a sound idea, notwithstanding). The general consensus was that this was a well conceived course of action and it would leave no doubt, one way or the other, about the origin of the rapidly appearing protuberances! As an added attraction, other surprises could be discovered. The major obstacle was how best to strategically deliver the 'waddah'.

Paulie floated the idea of use of a hose. This was rejected rather quickly because: 1) we didn't have a 300 foot hose; and 2) even if we did, Mr. Stannoni would probably trip over it and fall, prompting Mr. Rinaldi to call the police (and we would hear yet more novel Italian words from both of them that could be added to our burgeoning repertoire). Then Ritchie came up with a better idea—WATER BALLOONS!! Of course! So simple it was beyond brilliant! These clever devices were easily transportable, came in many colors, could be filled to produce different sizes, and, perhaps most importantly, they could be tossed at specific targets (in this case, protuberances) with deadly, pin-point accuracy!

So the plan was hatched!

The balloons were gleefully filled using the trusty water spigot in the alley. Each of us took 3, making transport a bit dicey. Bigger water balloons broke easier and got things wetter; small ones were more accurate, but often simply bounced off the hapless victim. With reckless abandon,

we opted for the *big ones*! Without doubt, they'd really soak that fiberfill!!
Paulie was assigned the duty of designated lookout whose job was to
stand on the corner and make a subtle, highly secret hand movement
(thumb's up) when Joanie approached the corner (our view was blocked
by Ms. Winn's big, red 3-story house that was rumored to hold 13 families and 14 dogs (a claim that was never verified)). Paulie stood with
his back toward us and he looked like he was doing something with his
thumbs, but we couldn't see. We had neglected to tell Paulie to face us
when flashing the signal! He became so excited that acting subtly was
quickly out of the question—instead he turned, started jumping up and
down, yelling some sound that was a cross between Tarzan and a coyote,
all the while pointing directly at Joanie. Joanie's quizzical look suggested
that she thought this behavior was odd, but then again, she knew Paulie
for quite some time and therefore everything was relative. We launched
from the Stannoni driveway en mass, employing a rather stiff powerwalk
(later, a physical fitness variation would be called dork walking) down
the block, hands behind our backs clutching *the* sure means of answering the fiberfill mystery! I was the first on the scene and winged a water
balloon dead on—

"Gaacckk!" screamed Paulie after taking a misguided balloon to the
groin. Darn thing didn't even break, either.

Ritchie launched one immediately, but it broke in midair and the
airborn wave hit the gaacckking Paulie in the face. Paulie was not faring
well in this adventure.

I unleashed yet another rubber orb of destruction!

"Uumph!" moaned Joanie as the balloon hit her right square in the
belly button, doubling her over like a jack knife. The balloon bounced
off and broke on Paulie's shoes, further adding to his misery. Eddie unleashed the next volley, splatting the balloon on Joanie's forehead.

"Thwapp!" followed immediately by a newly slicked down hairdo. Dougie was next, but in the adrenaline storm of excitement he let one wail over the bent-over Joanie, and the it hit the still-moaning Paulie right square in the nose.

"Splatt!" followed by more moans.

Seizing the opportunity, I unloaded a second balloon and it zeroed in on the area between the two orbs. A masterful toss!

"Sploosh!" followed by two more splooshes tossed by my accomplices. A veritable barrage of direct orb hits!

Joanie began wailing and screaming that we wrecked her new (white) shirt!

Our eyes immediately were drawn to two, quarter-sized, dark, rapidly growing tips of the orbs—very obvious under the wet, diaphanous white shirt (and bra)! I recall Louie saying something about the orbs and cold......Those things were definitely darker than the shirt now! Amazing anatomical discoveries! No sagging was detected.

"Damn, that ain't fiberfill!" I perceptively observed, "looks like those girls in the ocean from Louie Ferraro's magazines! Wow!"

The others were mute. Staring in amazement, mouths agape.

In fact we all stood there motionless—staring—some still holding unspent balloons. The only sounds and movement were Joanie's screams and attempts to hide the orbs and those dark tips (later identified as nipples by Dougie, the lexicon of novel terms), with her hands, accompanied shrill noises from Paulie's wailing and yelling that we broke his nose, this done while holding one hand on his nose and the other to his crotch.

We stood there watching this confusing but exciting spectacle for what seemed like an hour (probably closer to 20 seconds), whereupon Ritchie yelled:

"Uh-oh—look— it's Mr. Primaversa (aka Joanie's dad); let's get outta' here!"

Sure enough, there he was, coming up the block, doing something between a walk and a run—brisk pace, long strides, arms moving like he was from the march of the wooden soldiers! He had a cigar in his mouth and the smoke was bellowing out, this contrasted by his rather red face. We ran down the block, wildly dropping the unspent balloons! Legs don't fail me now! We turned at the alley, went through the yard and into the lots (undeveloped, wooded land [actually, more like weeded land] surrounded by textile factories). Our emotions were somehow teetering between sheer terror and laughter. There was also the yet to be identified testosterone flashes that we would later label, 'horniness.' We forgot Paulie, but Mr. Primaversa passed him by, most likely figuring that Paulie was an innocent victim of the hellacious water balloon barrage. We stopped in the lots to catch our breath and thought we were in the clear, having cleverly evaded the dork-walking, cigar-wielding, father of Joanie! We shared a few chuckles, but then Ritchie's eyes widened into a mask of terror!

"Damn! He's still coming!!!" he screeched, his eyes seeming to be 3 times their original size!

Sure enough, Mr. Primaversa was still in dogged pursuit—same walk/run, same smoking cigar, but now he was REDDER! Yikes! We took off into the wooded area and hid in the dense brush next to the fabled 'Monkey Tree' (a favorite hangout and site of many a tale of braggadocio, replete with a "fort" spanning some of the larger branches). There we stayed for what seemed to be at least two hours (only estimated, since none of us had a watch and we relied on Ritchie's Boy Scout ability to read the arc of the sun in the sky), until we determined that the pursuit was called off.

"Guess those things were real!" I uttered in sheer amazement.

"Nice boobs!" Paulie said correctly (he had joined us at the secret Monkey Tree only recently, after first having gone home to check himself out after the low blow by the errant water balloon). He was still limping a bit, however.

"What size were they?"

"Humongous! Size quadruple D!! And what about those tips?!?!"

"I like white shirts!"

"Yeah, especially when they're wet!! Ho, ho, ho!"

"Phony Joanie ain't so phony!" said Ritchie, proud of his new found rhyming prowess.

"Man...Where'd she get those?!" I wondered out loud.

"Hell if I know!" was the reply made in unison by the merry band of accomplices. "Good thing she was wearing white!"

Heads were nodding wildly, but in total agreement. A new degree of respect and interest was conferred upon Joanie, which also directly paralleled a marked degree of interest in those orbs! There was also a direct correlation to the increase in horniness titers. She was elevated to the level of a goddess! An electric storm of prurient interests was in the making! 'Whoowee' was the consensus of the collective unconscious.

Several days later, when the heat of the escapade had cooled down, our interest in Joanie had not. In fact, it was percolating vigorously. Based on some secret information from Joanie's best friend, Flattie Pattie (her name also being descriptive of her attributes—the boys of Fairview's interests seemed to be drawn like moths to certain anatomical parts), Joanie apparently had a secret crush on Ritchie, who until the unveiling of recent events, had avoided Joanie like the plague (insisting she had the terrible curse of the COOTIES!). However, after the water balloon affair, he was becoming a bit more open-minded and seemed to be rapidly developing a reciprocal crush of sorts. Besides, horniness always trumps Cooties!

Rumors flew, further piquing our fascination! Word on the street (from Dougies's brother to be specific) indicated Joanie went behind the guess-your-weight stand at Palisades Amusement Park and did "stuff" with Robbie Gartner (a notorious bully and voted most likely to be incarcerated in Sing Sing before the age of 19!). We were not certain what the "stuff" actually entailed. Joanie had also purportedly shown her boobs to Eugene Will (running neck and neck with Robbie for the first-to-go-to-Sing-Sing award). Joanie let an 8th grader touch her right asset on a dare! But most intriguing to us was the rumor that Joanie passed the word that she wanted to show her orbs to Ritchie!!

Ye gads! The opportunity of a lifetime! That lucky dog! Testosterone storms a rising!

Yet another diabolical plan was hatched, replete with a call for a witness who could verify the flashing and record it for all posterity! It was decided by a unanimous vote (Ritichie, Dougie, Warren, John, Paulie, and me, with no one abstaining) that the glorious exposure would happen in Ritchie's hallway. Dougie and I won the draw for who would hide behind the door to the basement, which was around the corner, but in a direct line of vision to the front door if you stuck your head out. Our assignment was to pop our heads out when other things had popped out (excluding Ritchie's eyeballs) and verify the sighting—This was truly a masterpiece of exquisite planning and attention to detail. Plus we would get a gander!

A Joanie sighting! Walking up the block, in a *white shirt* no less! A tight white shirt too! Momma mia! The guys scattered off the porch—several ran down the alley (yet another one of the many in Fairview). Dougie and I ran down the hallway to our secret vantage point. The plot was in play! The front door was left open a crack so we could document the dialogue.

As Joanie approached the front stairs Ritchie spoke to her in an obviously contrived deep voice, almost sounding British or something.

"Hey Joanie, what's up? Heard through the cherry vine (he meant grape vine) you wanted to show me a thing or two," he drawled.

"What the f**k is that f**khead doing!?!" hissed Dougie, using his typically terminology.

"Hell if I know!" I whispered back. "But he better not screw this up with the deep English voice shit!"

Ritchie invited Joanie to have a seat on the stoop and the plot unfolded, Ritchie crooning how good she looked today. Joanie was gullible and was actually falling for these lame theatrics. The deep voice stuff was occasionally interspersed with high cracking notes.

"Oh my God! It's going to happen!!" I whispered in anxious anticipation.

"I can't believe this f**king shit is f**king working! F**king wild! F**k! hissed Dougie, resorting back to his spectacular facility of cramming the most F-words into a sentence that was humanly possible. He even spit on the floor for added emphasis.

Very carefully and very subtly, in a slow, measured fashion, Ritchie crooned the delicate question in a velvet-like manner:

"Hey..can I see your tits?"

'No beating around the bush for that darn Ritchie!' I marveled.

"Okay!" was the immediate reply.

"Wow!" was Ritchie's response (although it now sounded squeaky and without an accent).

"Let's go inside." Joanie cooed.

"Okay!" Ritchie squeakily gasped in amazement.

The plan was going exactly as planned! It couldn't be more perfect! How diabolical!

"Holy shit!!" whispered a reddening-faced Dougie, expanding his vocabulary usage. A few more spits followed for yet additional emphasis.

Ritchie and Joanie came into the hallway and closed the front door. With her back to the door she crossed her arms, grasped the bottom of her shirt and LIFTED! She then peeled down the front of her bra. Ritchie's eyes must have gotten really big—Dougie's sure as heck did!

"Acckkkk!" gargled Ritchie as he stood there, frozen with this stupid look on his face.

"My God!" I blurted out as I sprung out of my hiding place and bolted forward to a place where I had an unimpeded, direct gander, face to face with the orbs! Just as I visually zeroed in (with Dougie pulling me to the side so that he, too, could get a gander), Ritchie's sister, Karen opened the kitchen door behind us and saw the spectacle at the end of the hallway. She screamed.

"Joanie's taking her shirt off for Glint! (By this time Ritchie had backed up and sat on the stairs, bug-eyed and wearing this stupid grin) leaving me as the prime voyeur.

"Rats!!"

The bra went up, the shirt came down, the orbs were tucked away in something like 100 milliseconds and foom—Joanie was history!

Ritchie continued to just sit on the stairs with a stupid grin and bulging eyeballs. Dougie jumped out the hallway window into the alley (all of about 3 feet below), almost landing on Paulie's head. Karen was calling to her mother, "Glint was looking at Joanie's boobies!"

"Was not!" I protested as I bolted out the door, turned left and ran like hell.

Mr. Rinaldi was watching the scene unfold from a vantage point across the street.

"Now whatta' da' hell?" he mumbled.

Again we regrouped at the Monkey Tree. Not much was said, each of the voyeurs individually replaying the course of events in each individual's mind's eye. The raging hormonal storms that had been fueled by the flashing, now subsided a bit, at least overtly. Covertly it was a different story. Plus we were terrified that Ritchie's mother was going to turn into a rat-fink (popular term of the era for someone who tattled on you).

No one spoke about Joanie for several days. Ritchie could not explain his taking a seat on the stairs and then mysteriously disappearing sometime after Karen did her Paul Revere impersonation. His eyes were back to their regular size and his Jersey accent reemerged. In retrospect, this event and accompanying fear may have plunged us headlong into Freud's latency stage, and the use of the psychological defense mechanism of repression. Latency versus pubescent horniness was the psychological mother of all battles!

Nonetheless, from that point onward, Joanie, (or at least certain aspects of Joanie), was the theme in many a boy-from-Fairview's daydreams…not to mention thoughts of a road not taken.

CHAPTER 17
Religion and Brief Counseling

Connie called to say that a Mr. Calvin Whiteside was on the phone and that he had a few questions that he wanted to ask me before setting up a possible appointment for psychotherapy. Actually, he called psychotherapy '*counseling*,'— something that people often do because in so doing, it seems that any given problem is less of a problem, there was really nothing wrong, only minimal intervention was required and things would be as good as new—pronto. I generally am not a fan of such phone conversations because they are an inquisition about one of the following: 1) credentials; 2) the possibility of negotiating charges; 3) which insurance companies would pay; 4) one's theoretic orientation; 5) my experience with a specific disorder; 6) whether I'd like to extend my already extended warranty on my car; or 7) other things. Without doubt, inquisitions are on the same level of desirability as a colonoscopy prep. Nonetheless, being a bit daring and figuring, 'what the hey,' I took the call.

"Dr. Wayward, I'm having some family issues and my wife suggested that I seek out *counseling* (arrgghhh—there it is again)," was the opening statement from Mr. Whiteside.

"Yes?"

"I'm a very religious man. A born again Christian whose entire life's purpose now is to do God's work."

"Are you clergy?"

"No, but I can only relate to a Christian counselor. That is God's way and that of Eloise. Are you a certified, well-qualified Christian counselor?"

"I didn't know there was a credential for that," I replied, "Is it necessary?"

"Never mind sir."

Click.

End of conversation and any potential of a budding career in counseling the born-again masses. The conversation appears to fall under #'s 1, 3 and 7: very brief inquisition about other things, after a credential and orientation check.

Too bad I wasn't a bit more mentally spry—damn 60's thing—I could have used some of the masterful techniques of Lester Finance, a true *Renaissance Psychologist*—one who is versed on every upcoming trend or treatment de jour. This man is the silly putty of psychology, changing his shape to meet the current demand, no matter what it is. A legendary divining rod of where the bucks are (except that I was one ahead of him with the feline owner therapy group. He, in response, had tried one with ferret owners, but mediocre attendance limited the financial rewards, leading to a rapid dissolution of the group).

If the call was for a humanistic psychologist—he was the most humanistic guy around!

Interpersonal psychologist—say hello to Mr.Interpersonality.

Sex therapy?—he'd certainly give that a whirl! (Plus he tended to be an auditory voyeur).

Hypnosis—you bet! Smoking cessation, weight loss, test anxiety, bunions.

Motivational psychologist—he was motivated as hell! Even made his own motivational CDs that clients could listen to multiple times in the privacy of their own homes. (at the bargain price of $29.95 + tax and handling—I guess the handling part is that he handled it from the cabinet to the client's hand). Rumor had it they made conversation-piece coasters as well.

His latest interest was executive coaching—a major need for floundering white collar types whose careers were swirling down the toilet, but who typically paid in cash.

Neurolinguistic programming?—covered.

Secret Life of Plants?—Sure, he'd read the book and swears he communicates with philodendrons!

Not to be outdone, Lester also advertised that he could cure specific disorders that were in vogue: fibromyalgia, OCD, bipolar disorder, ADHD, sensory integration disorder, depression, anxiety, multiple personalities, intermittent explosive disorder, Asperger's Syndrome, food allergies, animal hoarding, and excessive gassiness, just to name a few. If you have it, or even entertain the remote possibility that you may have it, Dr. Finance is the man to call. A veritable Ghostbuster of mental health! He was simply brilliant in his marketing prowess—unfortunately, less so in his clinical or ethical pursuits.

Lester Finance, BS, MA, Ed.D., CMFC, CAC, LCPC, MBA, APA, MPH, CCC, HSVP, etc.—he won the coveted award for most acronyms following his name four years running. Hell, his acronyms of qualification took the front and back of a business card! Guaranteed to dazzle the pro-spective client who typically would feign knowing what each of the letter groupings allegedly stood for, so as not to look ignorant in the presence of the erstwhile Dr. Finance. Lester also dressed the part—turtle neck and a corduroy jacket with patches on the elbows. Sometimes he wore this dickie thing under his v-neck sweater, sort of like an updated ver-sion of Perry Como garb. I think he used to smoke a pipe or at least had one sitting on his desk for all to see so as to add to the panache. Of course he sported the prerequisite goatee to round out the presentation.

I had a mental video of how the call would have gone had Calvin Whiteside called Dr. Finance. However, word on the street was that Mr. Whiteside eventually made the connection with Lester…

"Hello, this is Dr. Finance."

"My name is Calvin Whiteside and my wife suggested that I might be in need of a bit of counseling—I'm a man of God and I need a Christian counselor."

Long pause.

"My brother, you have come to the right place. Divine guidance had a hand in this phone call," Lester said in a deep, southern drawl. Where that came from is open to question, but again attests to Lester's uncanny ability to seize the moment.

"Are you a certified Christian counselor?"

"Almighty Jesus! I have studied this course of intervention and have been blessed with this calling," said in what appeared to be a Mississippi accent and adroitly ducking the question.

"I only need a few sessions."

"Spare the rod and spoil the child!" was Dr. Finance's response.

"What?"

"Be sure to turn the other cheek and duck."

"Doctor—what on earth are you talking about?!?!"

"Let he who is without sin throw the first whatever you throw."

"I think you mean 'cast the first stone.' You sound very knowledge-able—can we make an appointment?

Lester was on a roll—no turning back.

"God bless you and accept that which you cannot change. And change what you cannot accept. And give me the wisdom to accept change that is acceptable and changeable. (I think Lester was getting mixed up recalling a motivational poster that hung in the restroom adjoining his waiting area). I also accept Visa, Mastercard, Discover, and most insurances. Amen."

Weird thing was that Dr. Finance was Jewish.

Speaking of religion.....

CHAPTER 18
Mea Culpa

Religion was a major pastime in Fairview, as was evident in the behaviors of Father Mc Monty, the Ladies in Black, and the mission to have someone, anyone, (maybe even everyone) from the young, innocent offspring of each and every Catholic family become a priest or a nun. In the quest for that achievement, the first step in this ascent to eternity forever and ever in heaven for the young males was to become a full fledged, crucifix-wearing *altar boy*! Back then, masses at Our Lady of the Most Highest Extreme Holiness and Grace Church were said in Latin and every altar boy in Fairview and the world had to learn to speak that odd language that no one spoke except on Sundays, special holy days, at Latin Club gatherings, or occasional special affairs like funerals. To further complicate things, even if you could say a prayer in Latin, no one, including the priests (I was told this indisputable fact by senior altar boys) had any idea what the meaning of whatever you were mumbling actually meant! This was undoubtedly a unique form of double jeopardy! Sort of like speaking in tongues or something, although (except for the Ladies in Black) your eyes didn't roll up in your head and you didn't wave your arms around and stuff.

"Ad deum qui latificot…"

"Quia tuus deus .."

"E pluribus unim."

For all we knew the translations of these odd words could mean many things, but they must be good though. Altar boys were a trusting lot.

Now, on the other hand, give me PIG LATIN any day! That was a language I could understand and use with amazing skill and adroitness, the words effortlessly rolling off my tongue. Totally befuddling to the uninformed! In fact, we often befuddled Paulie and Mr. Rinaldi in our facile use of this mysterious, world-renowned, secret language (Paulie and Mr. Rinaldi were easily befuddled). Paulie had a very difficult time interpreting what he heard without us speaking very slowly and him writing it down. Unfortunately, he couldn't spell the words either, thereby making writing it down a rather fruitless endeavor.

"Ello-HA, Aulie-PA," we would say. Or "i-HA ister-MA inaldi-RA.". (secret code: first letter of the word came at the end, followed by an 'A', The 'A' was pronounced as a long A with emphasis). The secret code, allegedly started by Leonardo Da Vinci or Michaelangelo, was covertly passed from generation to generation, according to Dougie who said that his brother read that in a magazine somewhere. As usual, we were convinced and accepted this explanation as the absolute truth.

The look of befuddlement on the faces of the recipients of our secret communications was priceless and we spent countless hours speaking this marvelously mysterious language that only *we* could interpret! We secretly assumed that the original (but lesser) Latin was an offshoot of Italian, but not like the type that Mr. Rinaldi or Mr. Stannoni typically used. So it must have come from Rome instead of Mr. Rinaldi's beloved Sicily (wherever those places are). We heard that Sicilians had 'hot blood' and assumed that that caused them to sweat profusely.

Speaking real Latin therefore was an exceptional challenge for the young Catholic males of Fairview. It was a tradition passed on from one altar boy to the next, the pronunciations altered ever so slightly with each passing. This became particularly troublesome with the altar boys of Polish descent who had difficulty with words that did not start with triple consonants like pzk or wky or zwp. Luckily the prayers were on a folding card, however, that still didn't tell you how to say anything, nor did it translate what you were attempting to say. So there we were, put on the spot, right on the altar, priest in front, Ladies in Black and the rest of the parishioners behind you, all waiting for you to impeccably belt out Latin phrases. And you, being totally clueless as to what to say and what actually you were saying if you did say anything! Being the resourceful fellows that we were, we improvised. Basically, all you had to do was kneel, bend over so you face was six inches from the floor and mumble sounds that sort of sounded like Latin, all the while closing one's eyes, pounding one's chest piously, and subtly checking to make sure the other altar boy was pretty much doing the same thing in roughly the same tempo and cadence. I seriously doubt if any altar boy really got the Confiteor down pat. Eddie adapted and simply kept saying 'mea culpa' repeatedly until he hyperventilated. The less you know, the lower you go was the unwritten altar boy mantra. Some of the novices got so close to the floor on some of the more difficult segments that they had acquired red carpet fuzz around their noses and mouths. These Johnny-come-latelies were relatively easy to spot.

Going to Our Lady of the Most Highest Extreme Holiness and Grace Church to be anointed with our daily dose of religion exposed us to many behaviors that seemed a bit peculiar, even then.

In church you had to whisper—even if you and your mother (or another bona-fide altar boy) were the only two people in the entire building. It allegedly was impolite and everything echoed and God was annoyed by loud sounds. The upside of whispering was that you rapidly acquired skills in lip reading and in some cases, a budding career in ventriloquism. Pig Latin-whispering ventriloquism was really cool.

When in church, you also weren't supposed to point at anything because it was rude and that earned you a one-way ticket to purgatory on the express elevator. Not even the LIBs could prevent that one! Therefore, it often was extremely difficult to make other church goers aware of an acute emergency like if a Lady in Black's black veil had just caught on fire as she was lighting a prayer candle, placing her on the verge of becoming a blazing inferno. Instead, because of these rules, you were prohibited from: 1) common-sensibly yelling FIRE as loudly and as many times in a row as possible; 2) getting bystanders' attention by gesturing wildly, jumping up and down and double-pointing at the flame with both index fingers simultaneously; or 3) maybe even screaming and tossing holy water all over everything! Instead you had to whisper softly, or gesture with your elbow, the latter behavior resembling either a unique tic or the beginning of the sort of dance you would see toward the end of the night at a wedding reception, particularly if both elbows were used to point at the same time. (Actually pointing with one's elbow would later be a key behavior in the college drinking game, 'Thumper', raising questions as to the early religious experiences of the game's originators). By the time any help arrived for the unfortunate LIB, she would have been reduced to a pile of ash and melted rosary beads, sort of like the Wicked Witch of the West—or was it East?

Another cherished churchly tradition was that you always had to kneel on your right knee (genuflect) for virtually everything that happened in church. This included whenever you heard any ringing bell, whenever you heard the organ or any singing voice, every time you crossed in front of the altar (or even if you thought of crossing in front of the altar), whenever the priest raised something over his head (very tricky in the summer in the face of numerous false alarms when he was swatting flies), whenever you went to sit in a pew or left a pew (or even looked at a pew), and so on. Actually, it would be easier to list things that did not warrant a genuflection. The right knee thing made it difficult for lefties like Paulie. He only got the genuflection etiquette right about 50% of the time (he was often aided by good Samaritan Ladies in Black who whispered indignantly, "You usa' da udder leg").

Associated with genuflecting was making the sign-of-the-cross. *Everything* that was said or done in church was either preceded or followed by this four-corner gesture. Father, son, holy ghost (later changed to spirit for some reason) amen....A favorite past-time of the altar boy group was to have sign-of-the-cross speed trials. Bobby had the sign of the cross land speed record—150 msec (we estimated, based on rapid counting)— for tapping all four sites (forehead, sternum, shoulder, other shoulder) in turbo boost, warp speed succession. He could out sign anyone on a dare....sort of like a frocked Latin gunslinger at High Noon. Staring down any competition with his hands at his side, ready to launch as soon as the challenger as much as moved a finger, his nerves of steel and reflexes never failed him. Bobby the Kid—A frocked Johnny Reno! Simply awe-inspiring. (We were easily awed as well). In fact, Bobby was often so fast that at early mass, Father Winci, whose sight was failing him a bit, would repeatedly whisper from the altar for him to make the sign of the cross *after* he had already made the sign of the cross 4 times in rapid succession! We were amazed at his manual dexterity and blazing hand speed! He was once able to make the sign 49 times over the course of 60 seconds (unequivocally and precisely timed with my trusty Hopalong Cassidy watch). Unfortunately, as far as we knew, there weren't true sign-of-the-cross competitions in those days. That would have been great fun at church picnics or maybe at something like inter-church Olympics. Heck there could have been a mini-triathalon that consisted of most genuflections in two hours, most signs-of-the-cross made in one hour, and timed Latin prayer competitions where you had to say as many Latin prayers as you knew in rapid succession over the course of five minutes (again, not necessary knowing what the meaning was).

Yet another peculiarity was INCENSE! It was this really smelly stuff that looked like breadcrumbs, placed in a gold container with little holes in the top and then lit. This ritual released toxic fumes that often brought many an altar boy to the brink of asphyxiation (or even death—or at least wooziness or puking). This also most likely caused some type of brain damage that made it even harder to remember Latin. One time Eddie was swinging the incense in a manner that you would hold a Duncan yo-yo in the around the world maneuver (or maybe it was walking the dog, or the clock—again the asphyxia takes its toll on memory) the smoke billowing out of the little holes like Mt. Vesuvius (Eddie always insisted he did not put too much of the dreaded material in the holder, yet it looked like a smoke bomb) and obscuring the altar railing. In this dizzying, swirling, all-engulfing fog, Eddie got light-headed and this, coupled with obscured vision due to the smoke and his tearing eyes, caused him, in rapid succession, to: a) fall over Father Winci; b) crash over the railing; and, c) slide sleekly across the marble floor, abruptly stopping in front of the resident Ladies in Black who typically occupied the front pew. Amazingly, the incense holder landed upright and continued to smoke like a barbeque, the smoke drifting up the prone, cherub-faced Eddie's nostrils, undoubtedly causing more toxic damage, prolonging the coma-like state, and prompting the remaining altar boys who were still standing to flee for their lives (they had to scream in whispers and point at the hapless Eddie with their elbows). At that point the LIB were providing a serious challenge to Bobby's sign-of-the-cross land speed record! Their eyes were also rolling up in their heads, although it was difficult to determine whether this was due to the hypnotic effect of the rosaries, the frenzy of numerous signs-of-the-cross, or asphyxia. We were certain that Eddie could have used some extra blessings about then.

In the process, Eddie also tore his cassock, which was this red-robed contraption that was topped with a white frock-like thing. Sometimes the cassock was black instead of red—if this was the case, it was either lent, a funeral, or due to smoke damage from the incense. There was never any rule as to how often you had to wash your cassock and some of the items hanging in the cassock closet had to be there since World War I and never were exposed to soap and water in a washing machine (even an antique one). Unfortunately to do so at this point would produce dire results, the end product being a glob of material that resembled a red spider web. Some of those cassocks were a bit foul smelling, and this could not simply be attributed to frequent exposure to incense. Some actually had a hint of Old Spice—a pheromone used by many adolescents of the time, this typically obtained from their old man's medicine cabinet.

The bane of the altar boy was the 7 a.m. Sunday mass; conversely, the plum was Midnight Mass on Christmas Eve. The former often necessitated running to church as fast as humanly possible (sometimes aided by eating imaginary spinach before blasting off just like Popeye did) because one usually woke up approximately 10 minutes and 16 seconds before mass began. This caused Father Winci great dismay, the poor man gazing forlornly at the empty altar, waiting for a red cassock, any red cassock, to appear. Due to the eyesight issue he sometimes didn't see you even if you had indeed made it on time, perhaps because the red cassock tended to blend in with the brightly colored portraits of saints and angels and other really holy things. He sometimes mistook innocent parishioners for altar boys and kept telling them to come to the altar stairs. This was eventually rectified by the use of subtle whispers and moving of arms without pointing, sort of like a funky chicken. To compound things, the 7 a.m. sermon was said in Italian— the hapless altar boy was now confronted with a medley of languages, all of which were totally incomprehensible, thereby making the cassock-adorned youth feel like he was, for all essential purposes, on Mars (or some other foreign place like Hoboken).

In contrast, the highly-coveted midnight mass experience afforded an excuse to open Christmas presents *BEFORE* you went to bed, thereby preventing the annual tortuous agony of having to stay in one's bed on Christmas morning until the parents arose (which was usually well after dawn because of, as we discovered at older ages, late night beverage consumption that made everyone happy while assembling presents and putting them under the tree). This also afforded the opportunity of more toy-time before the dreaded pilgrimage to Cousin Joey's. The ultimate double bonus was the midnight mass/snowstorm experience—snowball fights in the dead of night, followed by hot chocolate and presents! Nirvana!

Wearing black cassocks wasn't totally bad, particularly if worn during funerals. Andy Fatlovic was the made-man of the altar boys, having a direct line of communication to the two undertakers in town (who allegedly were *real* made men who you were not supposed to make angry—they came from Sicily too). He also had a finger on the pulse of weddings (red Cassocks were the dress code for those events). Given that funerals were usually on weekday mornings, you had a legitimate excuse for getting out of school and you usually made five or ten dollars for being there! Tax-free! All you had to do was be nice to Andy and you were in! Unfortunately, Andy was a bit odd, so being nice was a somewhat difficult task. He liked to read encyclopedias for fun and although his family had a nice house upstairs, for all intensive purposes, they lived in the basement, the kitchen, den, rec room, and other areas all in one grand area without walls. They also cooked foreign dishes that smelled like boiling roadkill.

On one occasion before one Holy Week service I had been playing basketball all day with Dougie, Ritchie, Eddie and some local ruffians who even out-spitted Dougie! Again we were both amazed and intimidated by their spitting prowess. The court was up at the firehouse which also doubled as the stick ball field, replete with a strike box splendidly all chalked out. Unfortunately the strike box was quite large and put either short kids (top of the strike zone was above their heads) or tall ones (below their shins) at a distinct disadvantage. In actuality, the only one the strike box would help was the pitcher. But I digress. On that day, time and time again I unleashed the unstoppable Wayward right handed hook shot with deadly accuracy using the backboard with uncanny precision. In fact it was the only shot I had and I could only dribble with my right hand anyhow.

After a day's worth of the deadly heave-ho shots (and no lunch) it was time to join the other altar boys for some type of Easter vigil. Dougie said that a vigil was something where everyone was waiting for something to happen, but no one knew exactly what it was that actually was going to occur. So the altar boys typically sat in a state of holy bewilderment, waiting for whatever they were supposed to be waiting for. The first several pews (across the aisle from the LIBs) were reserved for this group, and we filed in, genuflecting every few steps and making signs of the cross in between each. It was an odd sight resembling a red and white caterpillar. There I was vigiling away while Eddie was up to his incense antics once again (Father Winci, that kind soul, gave him another chance and an opportunity for redemption). All of a sudden the angels in the dome over the altar looked like they were flying in circles and my eyeballs were rotating the same way! I thought this must be what we were waiting for—the secret of the vigil!!! Unfortunately, it was short-lived, as my eyes turned inward toward my nose, the angels (and everything else disappeared), and I was floating—downwards—this interrupted by an inconvenient 'bonk' as my head hit the wooden pew. Lights out for young Glint.

Lights on and I was in my brother's bed at home (his room was much more tidy and needed little rearranging in case of an emergency-in stark contrast to mine). Dr. Dannato was at the bedside with concerned parishioners milling about, Mom wailing that she told me to eat something before I went to church (eating was a universal remedy).

"If only he ate something—this wouldn't have happened! We're missing the VIGIL!"

I was out of the cassock and Dr. Dannato was loosening my shirt and pants so he could utilize his trusty stethoscope and check my pulse, and all that kind of emergency stuff that you apply to fainting altar boys. . He thought I was hippoglymented! (Sounded really bad!) I heard him saying that loosening everything would allow me to breathe better. Whereupon the cold air hit my jockey shorts and lo and behold my esteemed indicator of upcoming manhood rose to the occasion, forming a neat little pup tent of sorts—much to the chagrin of some of the female parishioners and a couple of the LIBs who actually left the vigil.

"Gasp, gasp! Oh my goodness! I mustn't look! Whatta' the heck is he doing?!?!" I heard through the muffled semi-conscious state that I was now in. In this rather blissful and proud state, I think I wore a wispy smile.

As I gathered my senses and the tent subsided, I overheard Dr. Dannato say that I seem to be okay and maybe my blood sugar probably was low because I didn't eat. Wrong thing to say as that was the impetus for another "he should have eaten something" tirade.

Nonetheless, eventually, the spectators drifted out of the house, each convinced that his or her contribution to the flurry of prayers had snatched me from the sinister grim reaper's grasp. They may have also thought the devil had something to do with the appearance of the pup tent. I was given soup with weird tasting green stuff in it (escarole or something like that) and was made better almost immediately, as evident by my loud and rapid retching and gagging. So much for the vigil, Latin, genuflecting, cassocks, or whispering for that day.

CHAPTER 19
A Session with the Pets-R-Us Kid

Next up was Nelson Winters, a skinny, 12-year old who seemed a half foot shorter than most of his same-aged peers. Nelson had a penchant for collecting pets, although that was not the issue that brought the Winters family in to begin with. His original presenting complaints sounded more like OCD—certain rituals, certain clothes, certain foods. It was certain that Nelson was a bit eccentric.

For example, Nelson had to bathe in a certain sequence—for starters, water at a certain depth, a specific temperature (he stole a pool thermometer from the neighbors), specific soap only (Dove), clothes arranged in a row, and the list went on. If something was not done exactly in the prearranged manner, the ritual would have to start again from the beginning. This often made for long nights, forcing the family to start the ordeal at 6:15 to allow ample time for 'do-overs.' On certain nights, poor Nelson's extensive tub time caused him to eventually emerge from the bathroom looking a bit wrinkly, the overall effect resembling a pale prune.

Nelson also sported a limited wardrobe. No socks with seams or elastic on top, this causing his parents to make endless forays to the sock areas of TJ Maxx, Sears, K-Mart, Old Navy, Macy's, JC Penney, Target, Kohl's and any other establishment that had a varied selection of sock-wear. He resorted to the low cut type (black) of a certain brand and wore them year round, even in blizzards. Long-sleeved shirts were also a no-no; sweat pants were primo. Jeans were out. He had a special liking for Grateful Dead t-shirts, being totally oblivious to who the Grateful Dead were. His food menu was limited: chicken nuggets (Wendy's only), mac and cheese, pudding cups, ravioli, and salami were the components of his well balanced fare. No milk, no cheese, sometimes chips and pretzels were okay, and juice in a box was acceptable (apple only). Presentation of vegetables or beef (other than a hot dog) sent Nelson into a melt-down, replete with gagging, wailing, and throwing himself to the floor, flop-ping like a tuna. He had to bring his lunch to school each day—with the same lunch items. Some of his classmates thought it great fun to secretly exchange items from their lunch bag to his when he wasn't looking—this usually resulted in Nelson gagging/wailing/throwing himself down repeatedly, much to their unbridled glee. They started calling him 'tuna man' because of the flopping. Nelson's food preferences changed every several months this providing other missing, essential nutrients, usu-ally right after his parents just stocked up on the previously exclusively-preferred foods once again.

In retrospect, Nelson sort of reminds me of Cousin Joey.

Nelson was therefore considered a bit odd (though a source of great fun) by his 6th-grade classmates and he was bullied a bit. He spent many a day in his school locker (after several of the larger males decided to put him there) or running up and down the school bus aisle attempting to retrieve his backpack as it was tossed from peer to peer like a hot potato.

He also chased various articles of clothing such as hats, gloves, and occasionally, shoes. A child psychiatrist had seen Nelson previously and felt he had Sensory Integration Disorder, which is feasible. Unfortunately, virtually everyone she saw was diagnosed with a sensory integration disorder, anxiety, and ADHD. Nelson was dutifully prescribed and SSRI for his anxiety, but was spared the stimulant medication. The meds and cognitive-behavioral therapy (not counseling) helped a bit.

Over time, Nelson wound up in my practice (Lester Finance's motivational CDs did not prove worthwhile) and therapy gradually turned away from these issues and focused more on a more pressing, long-term issue—an obsession with *pets*—LOTS of *pets*! Fauna OCD! He was running Noah's Ark!

"So Nelson, how are the animals?" I ventured as the opening shot over the bow.

"Dr. Wayward, only *some* are animals—most are reptiles and amphibians," was his professorial reply. "Actually, if you really wanted to get more technical.."

"No need for that," was my instantaneous reply. "Your Mom told me that your room needs a curator or zookeeper or someone like that."

"So?" was the curt reply.

Not skipping a beat I went for a direct approach—"She also worries that you hardly ever come out of your room."

"She should talk—4 dogs, 3 cats, 4 parakeets, a salt-water aquarium and wild birds out on the deck that she feeds every day—twice a day in the winter!" was Nelson's response. "Besides, I like my room!"

This definitely raised the suspicion of a genetic component to the pet hoarding compulsion. However, according to social learning theory, modeling could also be the culprit, raising the nature/nurture controversy once again.

"So what *critters* do you have in your room these days?" I asked, deftly avoiding another admonishment for not accurately defining a genus or species.

"I resent the term, critters—nonetheless I'll answer your question— Three spotted leopard geckos that eat mealworms, crickets and other stuff like that. I need to keep the heat lamps on them all night. Then there's the boa- I have to feed him 'mousickles'—frozen mice that you thaw and move around on a wire so the boa thinks they're alive."

'A dancing mouse marionette,' I mused.

"Then there's the iguana—he eats fresh vegetables and stuff, but he's getting too big for the 25-gallon tank. I have to put bricks on the screen on top to keep him in there. He's escaped a few times."

'No dancing tomatoes or lettuce at least.'

"I also have African frogs that I grew from tadpoles—they eat special food and little fish. Then there's the 3 red-eared slider turtles—they eat turtle food, worms, chopped meat and dried flies."

I suspect I had a look of amazement or intense interest because Nelson was really getting animated in his soliloquy.

"There are also 2 tortoises, 2 box turtles and 2 toads that I caught in the back yard. They eat all kinds of stuff, but the toads need to think the food is alive—slugs on a wire really get them going!" Nelson blurted out in pure joy.

I was losing count.

Then there's the hamsters and the guinea pig," Nelson continued, "you have to be careful not to change their diet too much or they get the runs."

'Good thing to know I guess.' I also wondered how many air fresheners were needed, particularly if some of the rodents did indeed have a sudden diet change. Did the Winters family buy Lysol by the pallet? Was this a public health hazard? Are a certain number of critters needed in order to be deemed a zoo? Questions, questions.....

"How do you keep track of all of this?" I asked in amazement.

"I use an iPad calendar to keep feedings scheduled—some eat every day, some once a week, some every couple of days. I used to keep a lot of the pet foods in the kitchen refrigerator, but now I have to keep it in the one in the garage—one time dad got up really early and must have been partly asleep, because he mistook the mealworms for granola and sprinkled them on his oatmeal. Dad woke up the entire house with this horrible sound. He's not too fond of the mousesickles in the freezer either—once he gave one to a neighborhood kid, thinking is was a flavored frozen ice bar. Kid took one look and screamed. Dad had a hard time convincing the police that he wasn't trying to poison the kid or that he wasn't freezing mice to be sadistic."

"Mom worries you don't hang around with other kids."

"I don't have time—Plus they aren't into pets like I am."

'Maybe the OCD stuff is not being handled as well as I thought—could it be *symptom substitution*?!?! I was also concerned that his social interactions were limited to running up and down the bus aisle in pursuit of his belongings or grappling with ruffians before he was placed in his locker.

"I am contemplating obtaining a ferret next," he speculated in precise language.

'Maybe he could rekindle Lester Finance's now-defunct ferret-owners group,' was my passing thought.

"Don't you have enough animals, er mammals, reptiles and amphibians?" I queried.

"I really want to get a TARANTULA too! It would require minimal maintenance.

'Make that mammals, reptiles, amphibians, and arachnoids! Another species—more variety!'

"So how big is your room anyway? Isn't it crowded?"

"I think it's 8 by 10 or something like that—Dad built me these really nifty shelves that almost go to the ceiling on 3 of the walls—so maybe it's a little snug."

'OMG!! (an acronym from my vast texting experience and tutoring from Alan)—Nelson's turning into a bona-fide ANIMAL HOARDER!!! That must be his diagnosis!! To hell with sensory integration! Ye gads!' I tried to regroup after that amazingly insightful moment.

"Getting back to Mom—she says she doesn't go into your room even to clean anymore. Is that true?"

"She used to, but…"

"But?"

"She used to until Wally greeted her at the door."

"Who's Wally?"

"Wally the boa—she almost squashed his head in the door when she slammed it and jumped backwards—blamed him for spraining her ankle when she fell down the stairs too! She got over that after about a week, and came back in but that's when the iguana pulled one of her escapes. Then Mom hurt her other ankle," Nelson lamented.

"I'm sure she would be delighted with a tarantula then!" I stated a bit sarcastically.

"They don't bite!"

"I think you'll have a hard time convincing her!" I taunted a bit, "So how many animals-er, pets—do you think is enough anyhow?"

"Don't know; probably never enough! Sometimes I think I don't need a particular new one, but then I see it and it's like love at first sight! It's all that I think about!"

'How poetic. How tender. Brings tears to my eyes,' I thought to myself in a very empathic (and slightly sarcastic) manner.

"Nelson, the better part of your day is spend tending these, these PETS! Before school, after school, before dinner, after dinner, before bed—maybe even after bed!" I pleaded.

"Yeah, I know Dr. Wayward, but someone has to do it—they need me! It's my calling!" was the matter-of-fact reply.

"Wouldn't it be nice to *not* have to do this all the time?!?!" I stated in a most logical manner.

"Maybe."

"Maybe?"

"I just said maybe."

'Who's on first—He's too young for Abbott and Costello' I thought.

"How can you go on vacation?" I replied.

"My grandparents come over—I print specific instructions for each pet and tape it to the cage or tank. Have to be careful with the hamster—he pulled the paper note into his cage a couple of times and made a nest. Luckily they fed him every day."

"What about sports? Clubs at school?"

"Naahhh; too busy—besides they don't have a pet club. An astronomy club would be cool too, but there isn't one."

"Wouldn't it be good to have more friends?" I implored.

"I'm getting to know the guys at Petco and Petsmart pretty well. They're my new buddies—even the girls. And they don't take my hat or shoes. I think I'll be a veterinarian when I get older—then I'll have tons of friends. Animal ones."

Trying one last stab at reality I said, "What would you do with all the pets when you go to school to study to be a veterinarian?"

"Heck—I'd just bring them with me! That's simple!"

'Roommate would be in for a surprise—hollow-eyed stare, sleep-deprived due to heat lamps and sleeping with one eye open to monitor the critters. Thinking he was going to wind up on a big boat with two of each species.'

"Well we'll need to discuss this more next week, Nelson."

"Sure thing Dr. Wayward. Maybe I'll even send you a photo of the tarantula on your phone if you'd like."

"Thanks, Nelson…." I said in obvious defeat.

I jotted a few notes and caught myself thinking back about the Fairview boys and their love of 'critters'….

CHAPTER 20
Fairview Fauna

Ground zero for Fairview pet collectors (at least the local neighborhood ones) was John's Pet Store (John was a very popular name around Fairview). This retail outlet could easily be identified by a somewhat faded, hand-written cardboard sign in the front window. The store was the size of a small living room and John and his family allegedly lived in the back, although they were rarely, if ever, seen. John always wore mostly white t-shirts and he had a hard time belting his pants because his prominent belly caused him to winch his belt well below his gut (essentially at his crotch), thereby rendering it useless. He forever was hiking up his pants in a futile attempt to maintain decorum, at the same time asking in a raspy croak, "Whaddya' want kids?" He was a poster child for suspenders and he may be the originator of the plumber's crack. John always looked like he had just woken up, partly because he may indeed have just woken up, was constantly rumpled, and also because his hair tended to stick out in unusual angles and swirls all over his head, this despite the fact that an instant remedy was close by—he was only a few doors away from Johnnie's Barber Shop, home of the all purpose flattop. Dougie insisted that John's hair looked that way because he really took numerous naps throughout the day while sitting in the ratty, stuffed plaid chair behind the counter and parakeets made nests on his head. Besides, he was a night watchman somewhere so he had to sleep sometime—it sounded quite logical (perhaps because we seemed to be the only customers whenever we went there, leaving ample opportunity for a quick snooze during the down time)— so we once again believed Dougie.

John's retail style could best be described as laizze faire –more of a hobby than a business. Hours of operation were sporadic, the used 'stuff' far exceeded new items, and the overall inventory was sparse. Prices on the same item varied day by day and John sometimes closed for a week or two without warning. This air of uncertainty prompted us to make impulsive buys lest the coveted item or critter: a) disappear; b) double in price; c) croak, or d) become inaccessible (only to be longingly stared at through the window) because John's was inexplicably closed again. This caused Paulie to come up with the witty saying, "buy it or fly it." He laughed hysterically every time he said it, and we did as well, even though we were uncertain what Paulie actually meant by this witticism.

The pet shop inventory included a few birds (alleged nest-making parakeets), occasional rodents (hamsters and white mice were big sellers), some fish (typically guppies), fishing gear, bait (salmon eggs and night crawlers were primo), and a large collection of used fish tanks of every imaginable gallonage (a word coined by Eddie that really sounded good). Some of the rodents seemed to live there on a permanent basis and some even had names. Due to transportation problems (of several city blocks), a typical tank selection would be 20 gallons or less. Tank portage was a two-person operation, and no one wanted Paulie to help because he couldn't walk backwards without sudden stops, causing the person walking forwards to sustain a jolting thump to the chest; if Paulie was the one walking forwards his stride was at least twice as long as anyone else's, thereby causing the unsuspecting backwards-walker to jog, typically stumble after approximately 10 feet, and also be rammed by the fish tank. Therefore most used fish tank purchases were made when Paulie was otherwise indisposed. If he showed up during the portage process, he was often given the role of a guide while the rest of us did the carrying (sort of like a Little League third base coach that no one listened to anyway). Besides, Paulie got confused with the left-right thing anyhow.

The used fish tanks were a gamble and John sold tons of black sealant that essentially was tar in a tube. Many a brave tank buyer wore the black badge of courage on his fingertips and under his nails for weeks after a round of attempted tank repair with the sealant. Damn tanks were tricky and many pieces of wooden furniture paid the price for an undetected leak, as did the errant tank repairer. The reason for the interest in tanks was we needed a place to store the natural bounty snagged at the legendary, renowned (and cleverly named) FROG POND that was located in the area now called the Meadowlands (but which we referred to in a more basic manner as 'the swamps'). On any given day one might capture fish, turtles, newts and salamanders, tadpoles, frogs and even snakes. Eddie was deathly afraid of snakes and if the S-word was mentioned, or, better yet, convincingly yelled out loud, he would typically set a new land-speed record to his home on his spiffy, English racer bike. It would typically take several days before Eddie would come out of his house after the b-line home, particularly if he actually saw a snake. Paulie would take great delight in leaving a rubber hose in Eddie's front yard after such an incident (he insisted it looked like a big snake).

Unfortunately, sometimes he forgot to take the nozzle off, diminishing the intended effect. Dougie, who thought this to be flagrantly idiotic, would usually respond to Paulie's humor with a flurry of disconnected F-words.

We used to ride our bikes in a westerly direction down to the Frog Pond, a several mile trip one way. The problem was that Fairview sat on the top of some pretty steep hills and we had to go through a mysterious place called the Heights on our jaunt. It seemed like a 45 degree angle of descent going down there. One had to apply the brakes and zig-zag for the entire ride, lest they overheat. If you went straight down the hill without zig-zagging, the end result was an unstoppable speed of 62.5 mph (estimated by a group vote). It was a true white-knuckle experience made even more so by the fact that if you didn't stop you'd barrel across Tonnelle Avenue, the main route for at least 100 different trucking outfits whose semi's resembled a never ending caravan of steel and black smoke. The likelihood of making it across the road unscathed was miniscule, so if the brakes failed or the speed of descent was 33 mph or better (our bikes also were well equipped with state-of-the-art speedometers), the concrete walls in front of the elevated yards of the corner houses were considered the lesser of two evils—besides, there was a chance that you might sail over the wall on impact and land on someone's lawn or hedges and survive. Indeed, Eddie actually did that once (he forgot the zig-zag part), however the homeowner was less than empathic toward the fleeing Eddie who sported geraniums in various stages of disrepair all over his body and who, in his bid to flee, attempted to peddle his bike whose front wheel was now the shape of a trapezoid. Eddie did not go fast. We also heard some new words that probably were the German equivalent of Mr. Stannoni's Italian temper displays, although Eddie steadfastly denied that he had defiled any ceramic lawn ornaments.

If the descending bicycle rider was lucky enough to stop at the curb and wait for the light to change, the cyclist then had exactly 11.5 seconds to madly peddle across the avenue of doom before the light changed again....this was particularly difficult with a trapezoid-shaped wheel. Wise bikers ran alongside their vehicles so as to save a second or two—plus you could always drop the bike and run like hell if the situation deteriorated. This experience undoubtedly spawned the idea for the later videogame, Frogger.

Unfortunately, we had to return via the same route, but now the zig-zags were necessary because it was impossible to get the Schwinns or the spiffy 3-speed English racing bikes to go up the hill vertically—made even really, really more impossible with a sloshing pail filled with recently captured denizens of the FROG POND! The world record for number of trips to and from the Frog Pond in one day was four, allegedly held by Ritchie (although two of the trips apparently were solo ventures, raising some suspicion regarding the veracity of the report).

The Frog Pond was an oasis in the midst of factories, warehouses, train tracks, abandoned boxcars, trucks, rusted construction machinery, and other industrial trappings. There were numerous channels criss-crossing the landscape and these contained dark, terribly smelly water. In fact , because the water was black we had absolutely no idea how deep it was. Dougie took great delight in seeing how long it would take a small fish from the Frog Pond to turn into a floater after being tossed into the channel. On average it took about 10 seconds. Unbeknownst to us, this was our introduction to toxic waste but Dougie called it poison water (undoubtedly poisoned by the all-purpose arsenic), and once again this sounded very logical. Paulie was confused with the term, 'polluted.' Unfortunately the fish floater trial was a sadistic ritual that we had to endure on each return trip. Paulie said he once saw a rat jump into one of the channels and its bones floated up in 5 seconds. This sighting was never verified despite Paulie's swearing on the bible that it was true—this latter action added a modicum of credibility to Paulie's claim, although several of us questioned whether Paulie actually knew what a bible was (particularly because he wasn't even an altar boy). Besides, Ritchie said that rats didn't have bones anyway and that the acid would shrink them if they did.

Luckily, the Frog Pond was not polluted and you could actually see things on the bottom—it seemed enormous but was probably 30 feet long by 20 feet wide—We estimated that it was 30 feet deep in the middle, this estimate precisely determined by the splash magnitude and sound made after a good sized rock was thrown in the center. John estimated the volume to be approximately one billion gallons. Since several of us couldn't swim (mainly me, despite my intensive training at the Palisades Amusement Park pool), we felt no pressing need to verify the depth— plus there might be very large snapping turtles lurking down there waiting for lunch to show up. We also were limited by how high we could roll up our Sears-Roebuck jeans. For some unknown reason we rarely, if ever, wore shorts, perhaps because Eddie's mom said that mosquitoes had an attraction to bare legs. We also typically kept our Keds sneakers on because Ritchie's cousin once said that the snappers can bite off a toe in no time, and Keds afforded good toe protection. We obtained sage advice from many sources.

Once at the pond, the ritual was the same: 1) Hide the bikes in the cattails (sometimes called punks; Fairview lore held that dried cattails (punks) could be lit and they kept away mosquitoes—punks also sounded better). We were unsure who we were actually hiding the bikes from, but you never knew who might be looking for bikes out in the swamps ; 2) roll up the Sears-Roebuck jeans (huskies could be rolled higher than slims). This typically raised the pants to one's knees; 3) secure the prerequisite fish net (typically purchased at John's Pet Shop or maybe even Woolworth's); 4) immediately resort to whispering and use of secret hand signals so as not to alert the critters (like they knew English or something), and 5) engage in a stealth-like, ninja-inspired approach to the pond, lest the inhabitants become aware of our incursion. I'm not exactly sure why we crouched down in a crab-like walk but it seemed like the thing to do. Paulie tended to mix up the sequence on occasion to the degree that the intent of the five-part ritual was often dashed—like when he crab-walked while still carrying his bike, thereby limiting his secret hand signals to only one hand.

The unspoken, ultimate, primo, quest for each and every one of us was the capture of the legendary, humongous bullfrog, Old Sneaky (again cleverly named). Slippery would have been a better name, but that was already claimed by the big catfish in Overpeck Creek. We did not want to confuse Paulie any more than necessary. Dougie swore that the monster amphibian, this frog-of-all-frogs, weighed a whopping five pounds and had eyes the size of ping-pong balls. On one such jaunt when Paulie remembered the proper stealth sequence, Eddie somehow got a bead on Sneaky, and slowly and methodically approached the critter in the proper, crab-like stance. His approach was flawless. Then, in a burst of blazing speed, Eddie popped up, yelled some high-pitched primal sound and swished the net down in a blinding arc, missing Old Sneaky by a good yard. The mega-frog jumped and so did Eddie! Somehow the frog jumped *into* the net, while Eddie screamed (his pitch was even higher than before). In so doing he let go of the net and Sneaky dragged it into the pond. This turn of events launched a frantic net-search (one never knew when John's Pet Shop would be open again to secure a replacement). Eddie was pale, looking like he had seen a snake, and now he was netless as well. Talk about adding insult to injury! Eddie denied that he had been scared by Sneaky, saying that he had spied a rat at the same time that he allegedly netted the frog. Old Eddie could sometimes think quickly on his feet. Dougie peppered the ensuing silence with an F-word extravaganza that undoubtedly diminished the likelihood of capturing any additional wildlife, particularly after Eddie's screaming.

"F***ing frog! Where the f**k is the f***ing net? Eddie that was f***ing stupid! It was only a f***ing frog—not a f***ing snake!"

"Rat my f***ing ass!"

Et cetera.

After a seemingly endless search, Ritchie spied the handle sticking up by some cattails, sans Old Sneaky. Eddie was now somewhat relieved about this discovery, though still visibly rattled. This course of events further fueled the legend of Old Sneaky, who now allegedly was 8 pounds, had eyes the size of tennis balls, hid in the depths of the Frog Pond (now a New Jersey equivalent of the Loch Ness Monster) and could actually grab a net with his frog feet and yank it out of your hand—attempting to pull the unsuspecting net-holder into the depths of Frog Pond! We all agreed that had we actually caught Old Sneaky, he would be difficult to transport home anyway, the added weight making the zig-zagging up the hill even more perilous. Besides, he would be too big to keep in a used, probably leaky, 20-gallon tank.

Snakes were another prize that could be kept in a tank. They were not as much of a problem because they lived in dirt, not water, thereby eliminating the leaking issue. The best place to catch them was the nearby" lots," mostly because we could walk there and simply carry the buckets. These snakes were smaller and less mean than the Frog Pond variety, and were called decay snakes, although the origin of the name is uncertain. Eddie never went on any of the snake hunting expeditions for obvious reasons. Once I caught four, yes FOUR snakes in one outing and put them in a tank on the porch. Mom was pretty adamant about them NOT coming inside. After they had been properly situated in large pretzel can, and worms and ants were thrown in for food, we left to taunt Eddie about the latest acquisitions.

Upon my return home several hours later after dutifully terrorizing Eddie, I heard a blood-curdling scream originating from the basement. I bolted down the steps, almost stepping on PC the cat who was quickly going the other way, only to find Mom with a broom and a large snow shovel trying to sweep a baby decay snake up—without much success. Boy could that reptile wiggle! Mom NEVER said the f-word, but I think she was really, really close to doing so!

"Get this thing outta' here—now!"

"Don't kill it—it's only a baby!"

"How the hell did it get down here?!?!"

'Wow—mom said 'hell'—that's really high on the PO'd meter! But that *IS* a good question—Maybe they can climb out of pretzel cans.'

I confidently strolled over and picked the snake up, whereupon it released what I think was snake piss, causing me to drop it and recon-vening another round of Mom, the broom, and the snow shovel versus the 5" baby decay snake. The snake was winning. This time I snagged it while wearing one of Dad's work gloves just in case the snake blad-der still had some remaining cc's of snake whiz. I placed the escapee back in the can to join its other three brethren, but I noticed there were now only two. Not good. I hindsight, I obviously should have used one of the 20-gallon tanks! Needless to say I made no mention of this to my broom-wielding mom, however the incident effectively ended my snakes-in-the-can phase of wildlife husbandry.

Easter time was another prime opportunity for pet acquisition in Fairview and neighboring towns. That's when the poultry store in West New York (a town across the Hudson River and sort of west of New York—someone again was exceedingly clever) sold live chicks and ducklings in the true spirit of the holy day. Ritchie and I rode the ubiquitous #22 bus south to pick up a few of these little critters—it was a grand idea, not accompanied by any grand design as to what we were going to do with the animals once we actually bought them. As it turned out that was primarily my problem because Ritchie's father, typically, a calm, gentle, empathic man, threatened to throttle Ritchie to within inches of his life if he even thought of bringing live poultry of any species home. Once again the derriere was cited as the target for breaking, underscoring the local fascination with harming that particular part of the anatomy. Only later would I learn what Freud thought about that preoccupation. As a result, our grand idea was modified as I sort of received tacit permission from the old man to make the acquisition—I asked him if it was okay while he was sleeping. The snoring and 'sssskkkk' sound could, with some tweaking and imagination, be interpreted as a 'yes'.

I purchased two ducklings, put them in a box, all the while dreaming about them sharing the wading pool in the back yard, swimming in little ducky circles. We gleefully flagged down a north-bound #22, whereupon we were greeted by a curmudgeon-like, burly driver with sunglasses that seemed too small for his rather large head. Unfortunately, as we put the coins in the grinding coin mixing machine, the ducklings started to cheep rather urgently.

"Hey kid—what's in da' box?"

"Ducks." I replied, resigned to the fact that the subterfuge was now a bust.

"Ducks?!?! What the hell are you doing with DUCKS?!"

Silence.

"No pets allowed on the bus! Unless they're seeing eye ducks! Har, har har!"

That was bus driver humor, produced by a man who had had too many busman's holidays. It was only moderately funny. Most likely, Paulie would have laughed.

"But they're in a box!" I protested.

"I don't give a damn if they were in a friggin' armored car—even if it was Friggin' Donald Duck and Daisy!" was the even less funnier reply, plus his glasses were now crooked.

The hiss of the opening bus door was the signal that this ride wasn't happening, forcing Ritchie and I to hoof it through several towns— luckily they were very close to each other.

As we walked the ducks kept cheeping. Over this somewhat irritating sound that was really beginning to piss me off, I wistfully asked Ritchie:

"What do ducks eat?"

"Canned corn."

"And?

"Maybe bread and lettuce and birdseed."

When we got home yet another reference to having something fall upon my derriere was made by Mom—this time a potential WHACK from the old man. She was obviously not happy about the purchase. While we set out to build a duck house in the weedy yard, I placed the two ducklings in a partially filled bathtub (it was too early in the season for the inflatable wading pool).

Big mistake.

How was I to know that ducklings couldn't keep swimming indefinitely? Heck it was only an hour or two! I returned to discover a face down floater accompanied by a rapidly fading sidekick. CPR was not helpful here (I didn't do the mouth part like they do in the movies). The remaining duck was named Henry –the name chosen for no good reason, in a moment of grief.

Because he was young and probably remembered I saved him from the ice cold clutches of the bathtub and I brought the canned corn, Henry began following me around. I had just read about imprinting somewhere and I was amazed that this could really happen. Right there in Fairview! Wow! Here I was—a budding Conrad Lorenz! This was especially delightful because no one in the neighborhood had any inkling of what imprinting was and they thought I was mystically gifted and had a special way with animals, particularly ducks. Sort of like a duck whisperer. I would proudly strut down the street with Henry waddling like mad to keep up, quacking like a son-of-a-gun! Billy Towers also had some ducks (lucky for him, his Dad drove him to the duck place) and I would bring Henry over for duckfights. Boy could Henry yank out billfulls of feathers with cobra-like agility! Even Mr Rinaldi was amazed at my duck skills and that was in itself amazing!

My swimming idea didn't work out—I quickly learned that ducks empty their bowels while they swim and it is difficult to extract blobs of duck poop from wading pools. Henry kept getting bigger on the hybrid diet of canned corn and bread, so the old man talked his friend, Beatsie (his real name apparently was Bob) into taking Henry to 'the farm.' Strange part was there were no farms within a hundred miles. In retrospect, I think I was duped, and vowed I would never again trust a guy named Beatsie! So ended my duck adventures.

Rats were a ubiquitous presence as well. These were not the pet type but rather the scare-the-hell-out-of-you variety. Some allegedly were the size of wild boars and they ate small dogs and stuff. Because many of the houses had now-unused coal chutes winding into the basements, coupled with an antiquated sewer system that must have connected to Rat Central, Fairview was rodent nirvana. At least my neighborhood was. They were Norway rats, although for the life of me I don't know how they got from Norway (somewhere reportedly very far away) to Fairview. Dougie said they hid in ships, but to our collective understanding , no ships ever landed in Fairview. Again, his argument was convincing nonetheless, made more so by the observation that they couldn't simply have walked here.

Rats loved to run inside walls and in attics. They also chewed stuff very loudly. This made for loads of nocturnal thrills for kids trying to go to sleep. This was the stuff nightmares were made of! Rats also liked to visit places that had food—like kitchens. This heightened the sheer terror value for kids whose bedrooms were right off the kitchen—like mine. Pop had a thing about rats—basically he hated the damn things—and with a vengeance. He didn't use poison because he said that they would die in the walls and stink up the house for months, and dead rats spread the Bulblionic Plague (whatever that was but it sounded really bad); as a result, he resorted to the old standby—rat traps.

During the colder months, Dad's unrelenting quest was to rid the house of rats, this made virtually impossible due to the never-ending supply from Norway and the numerous passageways into the basement. Nonetheless, each night he dutifully set the traps with cheese—he said if it was good enough for mice it was good for rats too (I told him my science teacher said peanut butter was better). The best place for the traps was under the sink where the rodents chewed holes in the wall to access the bounty of food, this despite numerous makeshift patches of plywood.

Each night I would try to fall asleep before the rat round robin would begin, but most times I was unsuccessful, and eventually would be lulled to sleep by the rapid, somewhat melodic footfalls interspersed with gnawing. I often coerced the family dog, Rusty, to climb into bed with me, figuring he would be a protective sentinel like Lassie. I was convinced that he would viciously rip them to pieces if they ever came into my room. Unfortunately, I often was alerted to his dereliction of duty by his loud snoring. At least he slept on the outside of the bed (I was by the wall) so they'd get him first. Occasionally, the old man's primitive trap would awaken me with a loud 'thwap', followed by banging and scratching under the sink. This typically launched an internal dialogue.

'Ye gads! What if his buddies come to save him?!?!?'

'Or worse yet—seek *REVENGE!* '

'How big was the rat anyhow?? Dougie said they can grow to 25 pounds or bigger!' And Dougie is always right!

'How would that fit under the sink!?!?'

'Wouldn't it get stuck in the wall?'

'Yo, Rusty, wake up boy!'

"Dad I hear a rat!!!" I wailed.

"Shuddup and go to sleep!" was the reply from the convertible couch in the living room (which was a much safer distance away).

"I think you killed it!"

"I'm going to kill you if you don't go to sleep—NOW!"

So much for an empathic response —it simply produced fear substitution. Shut-up or get killed—Weird part is I never actually saw a live rat. Pop used his work gloves to harvest the traps, putting the carcasses in Food Fair bags before I woke up in the morning. This fueled my confusion as to whether I really heard a rat or if I had some type of weird dream later to be known as a parasomnia.

My first gander at a live rat was at John (yes another John, undoubtedly a popular name) Hoppsbacher's house. He lived with about 20 uncles and aunts (most of whom were dwarf-like and all looked the same, this raising some genetics questions) in this big house across from the cemetery. They had tons of dogs and stuff (fowl, pigeons, a goat or two, etc.) that they kept outside in pens. There was this big storm sewer tunnel on the property that opened into a stream which then ran through the cemetery. Anyhow, we were in his crypt-like basement one afternoon playing with his train set that was well-maintained by the short, very similar-looking people. Suddenly there was movement in the ceiling rafters that caught my eye. There it was, nose in the air sniffing and beady black eyes STARING at me. I was certain it was about to pounce! A bona-fide, live, fat, grey RAT!!! A killer! From Norway!

"Yaaahhhhhh!"

"Glint—what's the matter?"

"Raaahhhhhhh!!"

"What?"

"Yaaaahhhhhh!!!"

Whereupon I began the fastest exit from the basement imaginable, falling over old, sleeping Sparky (the one dog not in a pen) at the top of the stairs. I was up in a flash, much to the amazement of several of the short Hoppsbachers who were sitting and watching their fish tank (they were easily entertained). Out the kitchen door and still going, I came upon the sewer stream. I was making a bee-line up the hill to Bergen Boulevard when, lo and behold, yet ANOTHER RAT came scurrying out from under some rock slabs. Now I was making a bee-line down the hill back to the sewer stream. I was convinced this was rat retribution for Pop's trap antics! It was a mass attack! I was trapped!

I ran into Hoppsbacher on the return trip and he tried to calm me down.

"I see them all the time—they're more scared of you than you're scared of them!"

'Like hell they are!' was my internalized response. 'They know what happened to some of their friends under the sink!'

"I'll get a stick and go back up the hill. If I see it, I'll whack it!" he said confidently.

'If I see it I'll wet myself!' I thought in a much less confident manner.

After a few minutes of rummaging around, Hoppsbacher triumphantly said, "See Glint—told you it was scared silly—har har har!"

'Ho, ho, ho …'

At about that time Anthony Pisterelli came sauntering down the hill. Anthony was an acquaintance rather than a member of the inner circle, but he was bigger and stronger than us and therefore was a self-proclaimed leader. Besides he had three older brothers and one was in jail! Dougie said he robbed a bank. Anthony lived in a compound at the end of Camina Street across from Pedodo's Italian bakery that made Italian bread and nothing else. Heck, he even had a rooster called Garabaldi—who we heard was named after some famous Italian bald guy named Gary.

"Hey man, what's up?"

"Glint freaked out about a couple of rats—not cool man!"

"They were big ugly ones that tried to bite me! They had rabies!!!"

"Weenie boy."

'So much for peer empathy.'

"Let's go in the sewer stream tunnel and see that secret room—I brought a new flashlight."

"What about the RATS!?!?" I pleaded.

"We'll make a lot of noise and they'll run like hell! No sweat! Unless you're a CHICKEN!"

'Oh no—not the CHICKEN threat! If I don't go now I'll be branded for life! Glint the chicken boy from Fairview. No job. No college. No girlfriend. Cluck, cluck. Think fast, Glint!'

"I'm no chicken! I'll even go first! Give me a stick!" I blurted out.

'What the hell am I saying?' was my immediate next thought. 'Maybe being called a chicken isn't all that bad after all. Better than a herd of rats running at me—beady eyes and razor sharp incisors glinting in the dim light.'

"All right Glint! You're on buddy boy!" chortled Anthony.

The die was cast. No turning back now! To run now would be di-sastrous. A chicken forever and a kid who doesn't keep his promise. A double whammy. A DOUBLE-CROSSER!

Down to the tunnel we went. Anthony, Hoppesbacher, Walter Cigolini (another peripheral figure), Ritchie, Dougie, and Johnny Askaris. (Many members of the newly formed gang were conscripted by Anthony after a series of convincing, chicken-implied phone calls). The tunnel was concrete and was about 4 1/2 feet high and 5 feet wide. About two inches of sewer water slowly meandered down. It was pitch black for the first 100 feet and it then abruptly took a 45 degree right turn. Then an ethereal faint light was apparent in the distance—it was from the ROOM! The room was concrete, was about 15 x15 and was at least 20 feet tall with metal rungs built into the walls up to the ceiling where a metal door was situated. Faint light filtered in around the edges. Several 3 foot metal pipes converged into the room from places unknown.

The origin and history of the room were based on speculation. Some said it was 100 years old. Others said that a guy was found hang-ing from the rungs –killed by gangsters! Other rumors held that several kids drowned in the room when a flash flood occurred or that hobos lived here in the winter. All things considered, it was crazy for a group of pre-adolescents to venture into a storm sewer system for no apparent reason. This again underscored the tendency for us to be easily amused. And not too bright.

In any event, the seven of us slowly entered the tunnel. It was like a human beehive. I was in the point with a wooden spear made out of a sumac sapling (we called them poison sumac trees—they were supposed to be like poison ivy but your whole body should turn red from any incidental contact although this was never witnessed first-hand). Anthony was peering over my right shoulder, his flashlight illuminating my ear. Hoppsbacher was bravely wielding yet another sumac spear to my left. The rest huddled behind us, some with closed eyes.

"Go away rats! Rats! Rats!! Go away rats! Rats! Rats! Rats!" we all chanted in unison, this rat-chasing mantra cleverly devised by Anthony at a moment's notice. For sure any unsuspecting rats in the tunnel were terrified and now scurrying away in the other direction at the sound of this marching, spear-wielding, fearless hoard of kids from Fairview! At least that's what I kept telling myself. I wondered if they understood English or just Norwegian.

I wasn't totally convinced that the rats were madly fleeing. However, I was moving forward without actually walking, propelled by the forces behind me. Stiff legged, the bottoms of my worn Keds simply glided over the slippery surface like miniature surf boards, the sumac spear pointing straight ahead. My eyes were mostly open. Mostly....

"There it is—up ahead—the ROOM!" screamed Anthony.

'Oh God!' I screamed to myself.

Somehow I had made the turn without being slammed into the wall. No sounds save the trickling water and the sloshing of 14 soaked Keds. Technically 12 since I wasn't actually walking.

We eventually reached the room and thankfully there were no bodies dangling from the ceiling. Unfortunately, this was not adventurous enough for Walter. Apparently the endorphin rush launched by the tunnel trip was highly addictive and Walter craved more. He was in the throes of what I would later learn to be a dopamine frenzy! Throwing thoughts of personal safety to the wind Walter began scurrying into one of the pipes and he disappeared in a flash. That prompted many thoughts.

'What about the rats?'

'Are they hiding in the pipes? What if they all charged at once in huge wave of grey Norwegian fur?'

'Where was Norway anyhow?'

'How long will Walter's Wearever penlight flashlight (with the little button on the end) work?'

'Is Walter nuts?'

Then we heard a blood curdling scream! It was Walter yelling for help! Ye gads—what to do now?!? I had a spur of the moment, excellent idea—get the hell out of here (and good luck Walter)! Anthony thought differently. While the rest of us cowered in the farthest corner of the room, as far away from the pipes as we could get, sumac spears at ready, he bolted into the pipe! With our main flashlight! We were marooned! In the dim light of the MURDER ROOM!

"Yaaaahhhh" we wailed in unison.

All we heard was Anthony's sloshing becoming fainter and fainter.

Another blood curdling "Help!" in a muffled voice—no it was TWO helps in TWO muffled voices, accompanied by banging sounds of metal against metal.

Then there were other voices—kids' voices! And kids screaming!

Then laughing.

Laughing?!?!?

Then more screams that were from the kids—raising the perplexing question of what in God's name were THEY doing in the tunnel and HOW did they get there!?!

Next there were Italian cuss words that were not from Anthony, Walter, or the kids.

Mr. Rinaldi? How did HE get in the fast becoming not-so-secret, secret tunnel?!

"Getta' the hell outta' dere or I breaka' you ass! You f***inga' crazy!? How did you getta in dere?!

Two things stood out: 1) Mr. Rinaldi, although somewhat comforting in his own way, was not IN the pipe, and 2) Neither were the kids. Actually a third (brilliant) deduction was that Walter and Anthony were in the pipe but somehow they made contact with the outside world.

We stood with spears directed toward the pipe, not knowing what to expect, our eyes adjusting to the dimly lit room. Then we heard more laughing and it was getting louder, as was the splashing. Then lights appeared down the pipe. Hoppsbacher ventured toward the opening, shaking spear first. He was brave.

"It's THEM!" he bellowed. "They're ALIVE!"

Walter and Anthony barreled out of the pipe, chuckling uncontrollably.

"Did you see their faces?! They almost pissed their pants! They really thought we were stuck under the manhole grate! Haw, haw, haw!"

Although relieved that the flashlights were back in the room and forgetting about the probable, imminent rat attack, we still were a bit confused as to what actually transpired. As it turns out Walter made it to a sewer grate in the middle of the Henry Street intersection. He also found a piece of chrome molding from a Studebaker and stuck it up through the manhole grate which happened to be second base for an intense punchball game. This immediately drew the attention away from the game, much to the amazement one of the players who happened to be standing on the "base." The pitcher, who, after screaming, made a mad dash home, just happened to be related to Mr. Rinaldi who, coincidentally, was visiting for a cookout. Hence, the laughing, cussing, etc. were readily explainable. Last thing Walter and Anthony heard was Mr. Rinaldi yelling that he was calling the cops!

That would take a lot of explaining and persuasion to convince Fairview's finest that the storm sewers were inhabited. The trip out of the tunnel was much faster than the entrance excursion. There was no rear guard as everyone was sloshing as fast as humanly possible, except for Anthony and Walter who still were laughing their proverbial asses off. Little did I know that the next rats I would encounter would be white (with little pink eyes), and participants in a Rutgers psychology lab experiment where they were given methylphenidate (a popular stimulant medication aka Ritalin) to see if they would press a little rat lever more. We affectionately called them Ralph and Floyd (the latter named in honor of Floyd Katsky, the biggest ass-kisser and cutthroat in the freshman class). But that's another story.

CHAPTER 21

End of the Day Musings (and associated Fairview Vignettes) #1—The Case of Bernie

At the end of the day on the commute home I would typically think back about some of the client encounters of the day (although there were some that I consciously tried to not think about). I tooled along in total anonymity with PSYCH 7 as my license plate. (Lester had SHRINK 1—he always called himself a shrink even though he wasn't; besides this term could easily be misinterpreted). Actually, someone in the state license plate making facility misspelled the first set of plates and the resulting PYSCH 7 made me appear dyslexic. I returned the erroneous plates promptly.

Today I had just seen Bernie for another session, having done so bi-weekly for the last two years or so. As we say in the business, Bernie was a solid, meat-and-potatoes kind of client. Unfortunately, Bernie was obsessed with games of chance —the Lotto, the Pick 5, the Mega

Millions, Little Lotto, Big Lotto, Medium Lotto, Lotta' Lotto—virtually anything associated with numbers, matching symbols, or variations on the word, lottery. He had literally filled buckets with that silver stuff that comes off the Scratch and Win cards (resembling radioactive coffee grounds). His latest quest was to make it big with the newly legalized video gambling. Unfortunately, this was not going in Bernie's favor either. This last therapy session occurred during the season that Bernie faced his demons—NCAA MARCH MADNESS! This was perhaps the most stressful time of the year for Bernie, being even worse than Arbor Day. He breathed, ate, and slept brackets—to the exclusion of virtually everything else. This was his version of spring break where he would take two weeks off from work in order to stay home and focus on the brackets, with minimal distractions. His wife typically took his children to Disneyworld at this time, telling them it was tax season and daddy had to work hard so they would have to leave him alone—even though Bernie wasn't an accountant—he sold insurance.

His co-workers dreaded his participation in the office pool because Bernie filled out an average of 64 different entries per tournament, while the 14 other insurance salespeople typically turned in one each. Bernie also whined, sulked, and had an irritable colon whenever one of his teams lost, the severity of symptoms increasing exponentially with the number of losing brackets. This definitely was, as we say in the business, a negative reinforcer for his office-mates (a fasten-your-seatbelt buzzer uses the same principle—you do something to make it go away). In fact, many secretly hoped he would win the office pool so as to spare them from this agony. During this time, Bernie's eyes routinely tended to bulge a bit and have dark circles under them due to excessive TV watching, frequent sulking, and lack of sleep. In the past NCAA cycles, he often sold household items during his family's absence (in Disneyworld) to finance his additional wagering with some unsavory characters with names like Bruno and Sal. Bernie now had to refrain from listing household items on Craigslist because his wife reviewed this daily from her hotel room in Florida. As a result, he most recently sold the lawnmower and weed whacker in the local Sunday newspaper. He figured that he wouldn't need them for at least a month or two. His primary care physician prescribed an SSRI for the near-obsession but Bernie tried to sell the meds as well. Lucky for Bernie, his wife kept track of things in the off season (time preceding and following mid-March) and maintained him on a strict Lotto allowance. Plus she had 'not for sale' etched on most of the household durable goods. One more week and Bernie would be out of the woods for yet another year—for college basketball at least. The problem was that Bernie actually sometimes won, this putting him on, as we say in the jargon-filled world of psychology, a partial reinforcement schedule. This type of situation is terribly difficult to deal with, because the unsuspecting client hopes the next time will be different— and sometimes it is—they might actually win once in a while. Hell, if the late B.F. Skinner could get small-brained pigeons to peck at a lever 20,000 times in order to get some birdseed, Bernie could pick at least a couple of the 64 teams every now and then and win a couple of bucks, or at least enough to replace some of the household items that he sold.

Looking back, wagering was another favorite past-time in Fairview, being right up there with religion and beer drinking. Almost every adult played 'the numbers' although during our younger years we were absolutely clueless as to: a) what numbers people were talking about, and b) how you actually played them. I do recall many an evening when I was sent to Nunngesser's corner to buy a copy of the New York Daily News from the somewhat shady newspaper guys who talked without moving their lips and were stationed outside Fritz's drug store—directly catty-corner to the Partview Diner. I never did figure out what you could get a part view of from that diner, except perhaps the neighboring White Castle that was down the block. This was not a particularly aesthetic view in my opinion.

Immediately upon my return home, the newspaper was routinely snatched from my hands by the old man who was almost beside himself with anticipation. He would deftly and with blazing speed, thumb through to the back pages and check the success of his wager. I laid low until I could determine if he was going to be euphoric or rip-roaring ticked off.

"Yeehah!! Damn we did it!" was a precursor to euphoria. This was also a good time to ask for allowance.

"Good thing I boxed it!" was an indicator of moderate euphoria. There was a 50/50 chance of getting the allowance.

"F**king piece of shit! Goddamn it!" was an ominous sign, usually followed by a request for a cold one. Even after provision of several cold ones, it still was not prudent to broach the allowance issue.

We were also introduced to the term, 'bookie,' which we initially associated with Fairview librarian, Martha Chiappetti, who held this position for 50 years, by our estimation. However, we could not for the life of us figure out how she would have anything to do with the numbers in the New York Daily News, even though she was really good with the Dewey Decimal System. Not until much later was this conundrum resolved by information provided by the source of all knowledge, Dougie (in retrospect, he was sort of a precursor to Google). Apparently, this was a very clandestine operation and involved the Mafia, FBI, G-men, the IRS, Elliott Ness, Georgie the Cop, guys who said bada-bing—bada boom, 'runners' (perhaps running from the bada-bing guys), paramutual betting (no clue as to what that was) and other terms that Dougie spewed out. We suspected that he could not actually define many of the terms, but they really sounded impressive, nonetheless. To Dougie's knowledge, Martha Chiappetti was not a part of the racket.

Another gaming adventure that kids could participate in was the annual Fireman's Bazaar. The purpose was to raise money for charity and to buy equipment, although the charity appeared to be the beer purchasing fund and the equipment was a new bumper pool table. At this gala early Fall affair, there were two rows of booths with spinning wheels where one could win a plethora of prizes, most of which were useless. One of my favorites was the Record wheel where the bounty was 78 rpm records produced by mostly obscure artists and which no one would actually buy outright. There were numerous Bossa Nova selections, marching bands, Enoch Light (not WMCA good guys material), and other albums that were even more obscure. However, my particular favorite was a Herb Alpert album with this buxom lady strategically covered with whipped cream. His band was the Tijuana Brass—we assumed that Tijuana was somewhere in South Jersey, perhaps close to Atlantic City. The album was cleverly titled 'Whipped Cream and Other Delights.' It was definitely an eerily irresistible visual magnet for pre-pubescent males who, in public, swore total disinterest in girls (another Freudian dilemma). Many an evening was spent listening to the melodic sounds of his trumpet, wistfully trying to see if there might be some enticing area not totally covered by the whipped cream. I played the album frequently—in retrospect probably too frequently.

"Quit playing that Goddamn bugle music over and over! It's drivin' me nuts!" bellowed the old man.

"It's a trumpet!" I retorted rather defensively.

"Shut up or I'll stuff that trumpet up your ass!"—This again referring to the apparent preoccupation with damaging one's posterior and the decreased likelihood that Pop selected the proper "numbers" that particular evening. Definitely not an ask-for-allowance time.

By far, the most intriguing booth was the money wheel, this attracting many more patrons than the adjacent booths where the prizes were towels, clocks, or kitchen supplies. One could bet quarters, dollars, or even ten dollars! There were dice on the wheel and if you picked a triple six and a triple six came up on the wheel, you'd get three times your wager! We were convinced that easy fortunes could be made here! The firemen were convinced otherwise. Although this technically was gambling, it seemed that the only qualifications for wagering was one had to be; a) breathing, b) able to count to some degree, c) able to reach the counter so as to place a bet, and d) tall enough that you could see the wheel and yell at the appropriate time. It certainly seemed like the Fairview police did not mind this charitable wagering around the corner, perhaps because of the patriotic red, white and blue bunting that was hung on everything that could be hung upon.

Patrick Buglioni, another denizen of the neighborhood with whom we occasionally associated, calculated the odds of a one, two, three sixes, etc. coming up on the wheel. We thought he was brilliant and that he undoubtedly was going to be an accountant some day. This feat was cleverly achieved by counting the total number of die on the wheel and dividing that number by the combination of interest. Of course simply knowing the odds didn't help very much, only that the likelihood of winning a 3-time payoff was about the same as Paulie going to Rutgers on a scholarship. This fact was difficult to explain to the wheel-spinning firemen who got wind of Patrick's brilliance and taunted us young wagerers with:

"So ya' think you got this figured out, eh? Har! Har! Har!"

"Hope we got enough money back here to cover those winning bets!"

"Oops—you lost—what happened to your big system? Ho, ho ho!"

It was exceptionally difficult to convince the firemen that simply knowing the odds didn't help to actually *beat* the odds, despite Patrick's valiant efforts to do so. The explanations were even more difficult after the wheel spinner had taken several "breaks" and gone back to the kitchen for 'refreshments.' I noted a direct correlation between the number of trips to the kitchen and the wheel-spinner's confusion regarding Patrick's explanation, calling the proper numbers, actually spinning the wheel in the proper direction, and providing accurate payouts—another precursor to a scientific mind with keen observational skills that would lead to a later calling in the field of psychology!

Dougie would typically attempt to capitalize on the effects the multiple refreshment breaks had on the happy firemen by slipping a few quarters on the counter just as the number came up. What clever subterfuge! Dougie's brilliant technique was simply astonishing to us—not to mention his daring! This ruse generally worked except when the wheel was under the watch of one very astute fireman, Bobby Moynahan. This cigar-chomping, ruddy-faced fireman (who was a good pal of the old man), had eyes like a hawk—no matter how many trips he made to the kitchen for refreshments. In fact, the only indication that he had made these trips was an increase in the ruddiness factor (we called it red face at the time). Dougie's magical movements, although judged to be quite good by nine out of ten observers, were simply no match for Moynahan's stellar powers of observation. On more than one occasion Dougie tried to slide the quarters at the last minute, only to have a meaty (and ruddy) hand slam down on top of his. Like it came out of nowhere! The reach was phenomenal as if his arm was elastic! As we stood at the booth and the wheel gradually slowed we watched in wide-eyed anticipation!—Ye gads-he was trying the ploy again tonight! And with Moynahan!! Holy shit! The wheel made its last clack and a barely-discernible blur of movement occurred at the triple sixes.

Barely discernible to *almost* everyone.

"A little late, don't ya' think, buddy boy?" growled Moynahan. "Tryin' ta' pull a fast one?"

Uh-oh—this doesn't look good!

"Whaddya mean?! I didn't do nuthin' wrong!" was Dougie's defiant answer.

"Pick up the f**king quarters and get the hell outta' here!" replied the ruddy fireman, who was rapidly becoming ruddier and using F-bombs with Dougie the F-bomb meister!. Dougie's eyes also noticeably seemed larger—my powers of observation that will prove vital in my subsequent career were continuing to be honed at an early age.

"You cheata' da' firemens! Whatsa'da madder wit you—they should kicka' you ass (there was the posterior reference again!)!" chimed in a spectator who just happened to be Mr. Rinaldi (who apparently had just come from the kitchen, even though he wasn't a fireman).

"What the f**k are you doing here?!?" bellowed Dougie.

This apparently was not a wise thing to say because immediately after doing so, two burly firemen appeared on each side and gingerly escorted Dougie down the length of the firehouse in several milliseconds. Dougie's feet were moving, but they were not touching the ground, due the fact that he was lifted by the burly firemen under each of his armpits, the end result being approximately a two-foot elevation. The firemen were saying things in Dougie's ears as they cordially escorted him out, some of which caused several of the ladies at the clock booth to wince a bit. I couldn't hear what they said, due to the crowd noise, the clacking wheels of chance and the gleeful cackling of Mr. Rinaldi. However, I concluded that they were not bidding him good night.

"Good bye Mr. Wisa' guy! No bazaar for you tonight! Ho, ho, ho!" he gushed. "Good work Bobby—you catched the sonna'da'bitch! He's a wisa' ass!"

Now the quest to break the bank was solely on my shoulders, the last man standing. (Patrick had lost three weeks worth of allowance a little bit earlier, causing him to wail profusely and go home to recalculate the odds thing). What a responsibility! I was trying to be cool as a cucumber under this pressure, determined to do this fair and square, particularly after observing the manner of Dougie's rather abrupt departure while defying gravity. Under the heightened scrutiny of Moynahan the Enforcer, I proceeded to place down some wagers.

After 14 consecutive losses, I suddenly came to the realization that things were not going well. The cool as a cucumber metaphor was useless as shit. I was sweating like a pig and my hands were shaking. Down to my last 3 dollars!

'Maybe I can sell my D.C. comics by tomorrow night!'

'This next spin will be the start of something good!'

'You're screwed Glint! Wait 'til Philip hears about this travesty!'

'What's money anyhow!'

'Oh please God, help me!'

It was obvious that I could do the internal, good angel/bad angel thing with the best of them! I was fast becoming a master of intrapersonal debate! This was what neuroses were made of!

'I'll go for it all! Three bucks on the 3 sixes! Nerves of steel!'

I stacked up the 12 quarters into three neat piles on the triple six—ye gads I would win a fortune!

"Goin' for it all, eh Glint?" said Paulie's brother, Artie in a rather sarcastic manner (I was also very perceptive regarding sarcastic statements since an early age, probably because I often received such (like daily) from my brother and other older acquaintances).

'Up yours!' I thought to myself—to do so out loud undoubtedly would warrant a pummeling from Artie right there in front of the money wheel! Witnessed by wide-eyed firemen who would dash to the kitchen to tell the old man his son was getting his arse kicked (Pop seemed to always be on a never-ending 'refreshment' break).

"Yup—all or nothin'!" I boldly replied.

"Then here comes nothin'!" was his prophetic reply.

Moynahan gripped the wheel so tightly that the ruddiness in his hand became less ruddy. It was a white-knuckle grip! He let rip a super-human spin that looked like it would last for at least 15 minutes.

Clack, clack, clack—the time between clacks growing longer with each progressively slower turn of the wheel. This phenomenon directly corresponded to a reciprocal widening of my eyes.

The 3 sixes were at 9 o'clock—clack, clack—10 o'clock—clack, clack,-11 o'clock!

'It's happening! One more clack!'

Clack—12-o'clock! STOP!!!!!

In what seemed like slow motion, the clacker-or whatever the hell the thing was called- clacked one more time—the 3 sixes moved on to 1 o'clock!

"Two deuces!" bellowed Moynahan, this accompanied by the launch of fine pieces of tobacco from the tightly clenched cigar stub. This tobacco-studded spray to my face further added insult to an already deteriorating situation, which was made even worse by the fact that friggin' Artie had his money on the deuces! It was even double-worse—Mr. Rinaldi won too! Arrggghhhh!

"Too bad Glint," said Moynahan—and I detected sarcasm again—no genuine empathy there!

"Told you moron!" was the nature of Artie's less subtle condolence. "Guess you better go home and have cookies and milk! Har, har, har!"

'What does he think he is—a pirate with the har har shit?' I covertly said to myself. 'I could go for some cookies, though!'

I was wiped out! Zero! Zip! Broke! Doomed by the Money Wheel! My life savings down the drain! No college! No house with a dog, a wife and two kids! I'll have to play the piano for food like Patsy. And I can't even play the piano!

I slowly slinked out of the firehouse, both pockets turned inside out in a fruitless search for a remaining quarter or two that could give me one more chance. I vowed to myself that this is the end of it—no more wagering my hard earned money. Better's Anonymous is the next step! I would stay home and look up the block from the living room window, silently observing the gala festivities from a distance. A terrible curse!

The walk home was a long block (luckily downhill). As I slowly trudged up the porch steps I was greeted by Mom who was on her way to the bazaar with some other members of the Lady's Auxiliary to make sandwiches for the hard-spinning firemen.

"Here's a couple of dollars Glint—go win something."

Woosh.

'Eureka! Watch out money wheel—Cool Hand Glint is back!" Besides, the wife and kids stuff wasn't that cool anyhow....

Move over Mr. Rinaldi—here Artie—watch how it's done!

There typically was no one-trial learning for most of the kids from Fairview.

CHAPTER 22

End of the Day Musings
(and associated Fairview Vignettes)
#2—the Case of Dewitt

As I ran through my encounters of the day, Dewitt came to mind. He is a pudgy 15-year old gang wanna'-be who could not be very convincing as such because of his white, upper-middle class background. To his credit, he sported the right look—flat bill ball cap worn strategically at a 45 degree angle from his nose, still with the price tag attached. He wore the prerequisite baggy pants in which he could have secretly smuggled several small people across state lines, if he were so inclined. The clothing ensemble was topped off with Shaq/Rodman/LeBron/Jordan/ Bob Cousey combo basketball shoes that each weighed approximately the same as a cinderblock. He used his hands in an intriguing manner—various fingers pointing in various directions at various angles, all simultaneously. Apparently, these well-choreographed movements were designed to add emphasis and clarity to his communications, the verbal component being approximately 15% intelligible. He obviously spent many hours in front of the mirror perfecting this technique. Lately, Dewitt had been dabbling in various illicit substances. This week's escapade involved inhalants, more specifically, 'huffing.' Rather than use paint or other popular solvents, Dewitt cleverly elected to use Glade air freshener as it was easily obtainable at the local Walmart. He was discovered because every time he walked past his parents his eyes were red and they kept smelling rose petals. Initially they thought he had a new cologne, but Dewitt didn't wear cologne and he would have had to be afflicted with a sudden case of conjunctivitis to explain the red-eye phenomenon. The session brought back memories of early dabbling in alcohol by the boys of Fairview.

Living in Fairview (and neighboring boroughs), we were introduced to alcohol at an early age—roughly about age 4. Many Italian families supplied their young offspring with a small glass of wine at dinner time, the rationale being that is was good for them. Since I came from an Irish-Italian gene pool and we lived in an Italian-owned house, the time-honored tradition was still practiced. However, because of the hybrid ethnicity, the Wayward family improvised and I was given a small glass of Knickerbocker beer, again because it was purportedly good for me. In retrospect, I think my parents and grandparents simply wanted me to go to sleep early.

Moving on, one had to be 21 to imbibe in New Jersey, but 18 to quaff a few in the bordering state, New York (dramatically increasing our interstate commerce in our later teen years). One could be even younger if the right establishment was selected and proper ID was fetched from one's wallet (called getting proofed). Paulie, despite his large size, once tried to use his Lincoln school eighth grade ID card (he was in high school by then)—he was quickly dispatched out of the local package goods store by a broom-wielding clerk. His ID was definitely not proper. Paulie never quite grasped the 'proper' thing.

We initially started our early high school alcohol experimentation via the age-old, time-honored tradition of pilfering. Early favorites were Old Overhalt whiskey, lifted from Larry Garangello's basement and hidden in a secret place in a lot across from the high school. Another excellent choice was Old Bohemian beer, a prized selection from Mike Gratellini's basement (we quickly discovered that basements were a fine source of oddly named, terrible-tasting alcoholic beverages). Early on, having a sip or two made it perfectly acceptable to claim you were drunk and act like a Bozo. Larry apparently had a very fast metabolic rate, because immediately (5 milliseconds) after he took a sip, the Bozoidedness often would begin.

As we aged, our liquor acquisition techniques became more brazen and bordered on reckless abandon. One such technique was to engage in interstate commerce and take the Orange and Black bus across the George Washington Bridge to Acropolis Liquors, which contained a veritable cornucopia of alcoholic beverages. This was made more daring and brazen because of the interstate component and the possibility of FBI involvement. The prerequisite for being able to purchase alcohol at Acropolis apparently was dependent on one's ability to be able to look over the counter without standing on one's tippy-toes (the counter also was relatively low). We began this practice around age 16 (when most of us could easily have passed for 12). We typically used the even-odds technique to decide the courier of the day. According to Dougie, this age-old practice allegedly was started in the 1700's by the Pilgrims— one of the participants would yell '1-2-3-shoot' and the two contestants would quickly put out one or two fingers—the resulting sum being even or odd. I later learned this was a simpler version of rock-paper-scissors, this more easily mastered by the Fairview boys due to the lesser number of choices that were involved. Nonetheless, Paulie never truly appreciated which combinations were even or odd and he would always believe the call made by his opponent. Hence he would lose consistently. The only problem was that he would always forget what he was supposed to buy when he arrived at Acropolis, so he was usually exempt from the 1-2-3-shoot selection process. It was the zenith of manhood, when at the ripe age of 16, one would ride back across the gateway, George Washington Bridge, right past the toll booths, with a highly illegal paper bag stuffed with clanking bottles, and embark from the bus to be greeted by the cheering hoard (actually two or three co-conspirators) who had been anxiously waiting at the bus stop. The feeling of pride was as if you had just returned from the moon (well, it was another state at least).

One very memorable drinking event was the late summer gathering of the guys before some of us went away to college. This also signaled the next big step in our journey through life. Larry convinced us that a superb summer refresher to toast our temporary parting of ways was vodka and grape juice. Plus it was somewhat nutritious. Despite puberty, we were still easily convinced. We did the usual bus procedure (no one wanted to drive across the bridge) and Larry, Mike, John, Dave Freedwitz, Wesley (now not resembling a cheese doodle despite continued misadventures in tanning) and I did the even-odds thing and I lost to everyone—therefore I was the designated, highly illegal transporter. I left with the encouraging cheers of my buddies ringing in my ears.

"Go Glint!"

"Acropolis here we come!"—I didn't get the 'we' part.

"Pax vobiscum!"—a carry over from the altar boy days.

Et cetera.

The ride was quick and the store was only a block away from the bus stop. I sauntered into the establishment, thoughts of vodka and grape-juice dancing in my head.

"Whadda' ya' want buddy?"

" Two fifths of Seagrams vodka." I said in a deep voice.

"You 18?"

' OMG—they NEVER asked that before! Ye gads! The game is over! I'm going to Sing-Sing! No college for you bucko!'

'Wait, get hold of yourself—you're Glint Wayward and you have to do this for your buddies!'

'Screw them—I'm the one going to jail!'

Somewhere during the throes of my internal dialogue, automatic pilot took over.

"Sure—and I got a draft card" (it wasn't actually a real, bonafide draft card but Tony Cappasso would get it somewhere and would type your name on it and it only cost five bucks—rumor had it Tony also ran numbers. Tony was an unusual guy—well dressed, spit like a pro, 'connected,' but he couldn't climb the ropes in gym class—he typically just hung there like a dead tuna and turned really red. However, nobody laughed at the hilarious spectacle of the dangling red tuna lest Tony call in a favor. Back to Acropolis.

"Let's see it buddy."

I handed the card over with feigned self-confidence (after all, Tony's forgery was never put to the test) and he looked at it for a total of 8 nanoseconds and gave it back. I guess the proximity to the bus stop in his mind made it unlikely that I had a driver's license. He retrieved the two bottles, bagged them up and took the money (actually I had about eight dollars in quarters from Wesley's contribution to our purchase). I caught the westbound bus, sat in the back, and crossed over the Hudson

River (source of Palisade's Amusement Parks salt water), all the while the tightly clutching the bundle in my lap. I triumphantly debarked from the bus at the first Jersey stop. I was greeted by the appreciative smiles and whoops of my soon-to-be-grapejuice-and-vodka-imbibing pals who were sitting in anxious anticipation in Larry's father's rusty Comet. The car was idling but it sounded like a lawn mower. Mike raised up the bottles of grape juice as if he had just won two Oscars.

Mike came up with the idea that we should toast this educational milestone in front of the high school—after all this is where we spent the last couple of years preparing for our future! What could be more fitting!? We left Larry's car parked a few blocks away so as to not draw attention, although in the process, many heads appeared in windows of surrounding houses in an effort to determine who would be mowing a lawn in the dark.

We did a preparation check:

"Plastic cups?"

"Yep".

"Vodka?"

"Got it—grape juice too!"

"How do we mix this?"

"Hell if I know!"

"Half and half" piped up Wesley.

"I read it somewhere," was his response to Dave's skeptical expression of 'how in the hell do you know that?' Wesley had been editor of the school newspaper and he was going to major in journalism, so we assumed that he did read a lot, so it was feasible that he probably did encounter this recipe somewhere. He proceeded to gleefully mix the proper components, and proudly offered the fruit of his effort to Dave who quickly gulped it down.

"Aaack—gaaccckkk—gasp—mmm-mmm good!" rasped Dave.

With that, we all began quaffing the expertly made concoction.

'Mmmm-mmmm good my ass" I thought. 'This is freakin' terrible!' I have heard people say that certain drinks taste like piss (such as warm Old Bohemian beer), but always wondered how they actually knew what piss tasted like. Not having actually sampled it firsthand, I nonetheless suspect that piss might taste like grapejuice and vodka. However, I must admit the taste seemed to improve with each gulp. The revelry went on for quite some time, the ratio of intelligent conversation to idiocy deteriorating by the minute. We also had more vodka than grapejuice, so the 50/50 mix was now a 70/30 blend, favoring the former ingredient. Sitting at the bottom of the high school stairs at a busy, four-way intersection was also not a particularly good idea either—this impression was further supported by the fact that the streetlight was directly above us.

Dave was the first casualty—while engaged in nonsensical dialogue (and us listening closely) he stopped in mid-sentence and bolted toward the curb with pretty amazing speed. Luckily he stopped just before he went head first into traffic—however a torrent of purple-colored liquid was launched and that *did* go into traffic!

"Barrfff—gaacckkk—uggghhhh- splash" Dave made heretofore unheard of sounds, the timbre and cadence suggesting that he might suddenly have become possessed. The event was quite startling. These sequences of sounds, replete with what seemed like gallons of purple liquid and other debris, were repeated at least five times in rapid succession (Mike later told us he was keeping count). It was amazing that Dave was able to hold that much to begin with! Wesley insisted that he had read that the stomach can expand 10 times its normal size when alcohol was involved. Again, since he read a lot, we accepted this explanation.

His level of persuasion was on par with Dougie! The overhead streetlight illuminated this spectacle nicely, especially the purple part.

Unfortunately, Dave's barf of infamy caught the eye of a local police officer who just happened to be cruising by, his attention further solicited by the purple splotch that suddenly appeared on his right front fender.

Red and blue lights on. Several short siren bursts.

"Oh shit!" we blurted out in unison.

"Barrrffff—uggghhhhh" Dave blurted out in solo.

"What are you boys doing over there? Don't move!" the officer boomed through the loudspeaker.

"Double oh shit!" I whispered.

"Nothin' officer," was Dave's slurred reply, accompanied by a smile and then more purple vomit.

The volume that that kid held was utterly amazing by any standard!

"What's in the cups?"

"Grapejuice!!!"

"Grapejuice my ass!"(again the reference to one's buttocks). "You guys are drinking—pour it on the ground—NOW!"

Larry and John had witnessed the scene unfolding and at the first sign of Dave's folly, hid behind some trees, unbeknownst to the police officer. That left Dave, Wesley, Mike and I to deal with the wrath of the law.

"Get your sorry asses in the car!" bellowed the tall, rather lanky police officer as he opened the back door of the cruiser (again the Freudian fascination with bums). We meekly began to pile in with Dave (whose t-shirt now sported a purple bib of sorts) as the lead man.

Then I saw IT! In the center of the back seat, illuminated by the streetlight, was a pristine, brand-new police summer-issue, Mountie hat. Wesley saw it too and whispered that he had read a recent news story announcing this spiffy addition to the Cliffside Park police summer ensemble. We were not impressed with Wesley's knowledge at this point in time. Dave, unfortunately, didn't see the hat and plopped right smack dead center on the crown, flattening it like a pancake.

'We're doomed! Shit! A felt Frisbee! He's going to shoot us!'

"Hey—put the hat on the rear deck and be damn careful!" snorted officer Grim!

"Yes sir! We all chimed in except Dave who was totally unaware of: a) the gravity of the current situation, b) where he was, and c) the lump under his rear end. I subtly edged the hat from under Dave and attempted to pop the crown back out, with a modicum of success. It now resembled a lopsided Idaho potato on a brown plate, which was much better than a pancake in my estimation, and deserving of less time in jail. The ride to the station was a short one, made a bit faster by Officer Grim's tendency to step on the accelerator for forcefully in response to each false barf alarm from Dave.

As we piled out of the back seat I meekly handed Officer Grim (the nickname I, in an impromptu fashion, cleverly devised) his semi-repaired Mountie hat.

"Thanks kid—hey what the f**k did you do to this?!?! Wise guys, eh?!? Get the f**k in the station—NOW!" he growled in a manner not fitting for an officer of the peace. His veins were sticking out by his temples, made more obvious because he wasn't wearing a hat. When he did put it on he looked rather comical. This would have caused hysterical laughing had not the situation been so dire.

We entered the station and the Sergeant was sitting on this platform-like desk that must have been perched eight feet high—it reminded me of the Wizard of Oz. I think it was built that way to intimidate those who stood before it. It certainly was working. The four of us stood there, minimally swaying, except for Dave and now, Wesley.

"Sarge—caught them drinking in front of the high school—this one was puking."

"What's the matter with your hat? Looks crooked-what did ya' do sit on it?" queried the Sergeant.

'Oh shit' I thought as Officer Grim menacingly glared at his quarry.

The Sarge peered over his reading glasses and his eyebrows raised. "Hey—aren't you Glint Wayward—Phil's son?"

"Yes sir."

"What the hell are you doing? I'm gonna' tell your old man and he's going to kick your ass!"

Several thoughts ran through my mind: a) there's the ass reference again, b) he knows the old man, and c) he's right—the old man is going to kill me! We told him about the celebration, indicated that none of us was driving, spoke about college, whined profusely, and in general put on a rather pathetic show, accompanied by periodic dry heaves from Dave. Luckily, Sarge Kelsey was a drinking buddy of the old man and they spent many an evening at Gil's tavern. He told us to get the hell out of his station and if we got hauled in again he was going to lock us up over night!

Officer Grim glared at us as we left, and Sarge Kelsey was right—his hat was definitely still crooked.

We stumbled to Larry's house which was about two miles away—the stumbling due to the effects of the alcohol, the delayed traumatic factor of being hauled into the police station, and general fatigue. Larry and John had retrieved the Comet and were sitting on the porch, their raucous laughing amplified by the effect of narrow streets lined with closely situated houses on postage-stamp sized lots. Next to them was Larry's inert basset hound, Penny, who in a natural observation experiment spontaneously devised by Larry and John, was given some Old Overhalt and Coke to see what a drunken basset hound would do. They found that drunken basset hounds don't do much except lay there on their back and make moaning sounds.

Reunited, we all celebrated our good fortune. Unfortunately, Dave was not in a celebratory mood and, in fact, immediately fell asleep on the lawn after a less-than-graceful face-plant. Wesley now did the sudden bolt-to-the-curb thing and viola—another torrent of purple mush, the velocity definitely on par with Dave's! When he turned around we made a startling discovery. Wesley was missing a front tooth—he looked sort of like a jack-o-lantern!

"Wes—where's your front tooth?" I asked.

"Don't tell me you're drunk too!" grumbled John, who was now bored with the inert basset hound experiment.

"What tooth?" Wesley slurred quizzically.

"The tooth that's not there!"

"Oh that tooth—it's false—what— it's not there?!?!? Shit!"

"Damn Glint, you're right! John said in an incredulous manner, all the while staring at Wesley's now-asymmetric smile.

Wesley launched into the puddle of purple liquid, frantically clawing to the right and then to the left, in search of his missing false tooth that heretofore he had us believe was au natural. It was not a pretty sight.

"I found it! I found it!" he boomed after only a minimal amount of time, whereupon he vomited again.

As if on cue, Larry's father came out on the porch to see what the ruckus was. Being both perceptive and not drunk, his gaze riveted on Wesley who was kneeling in the purple puddle. "What the hell is that?"

Larry, with amazing quickness of mind (despite the vodka and grapejuice) said, "the dog puked!" Penny's continued inertia and occasional moans added credibility to his claim. "I think she's sick."

"What the hell did she eat that was purple? And why the hell are you kneeling in it?!" were Mr. Garangello's suspicious, but insightful questions.

Before Larry could answer, Mr. Garangello's focus shifted to Wesley's face.

"Where's your tooth son? You in a fight?"

"No sir, crown broke."

"Weird shit going on here—I'm going to bed. Clean up that stuff, whatever it is!"

So ended the night of pre-college revelry.

Larry got a hose.

Dave finally woke up, stood, and then fell in the hedges.

Larry hosed Dave off after he first addressed the purple puddle.

Mike and John strolled off pondering the reasons for their failed experiment.

I thanked God for Gil's tavern all the way home

Wesley put his tooth in his pocket and proceeded to talk without moving his lips.

Penny still was inert but the moaning had subsided. She seemed to be smiling.

All in all, a rather dubious beginning to life away from the place we called home.

CPSIA information can be obtained
at www.ICGtesting.com
Printed in the USA
LVOW10s0108200418
574225LV00010B/268/P